Praises for
Laying Down the Law

I appreciate not only Dr. Halsey's writing style and wit in his book, *Laying Down the Law*, but even more his clarity on the gospel of grace and interaction with the text of Scripture. He clarifies that the law can neither justify the sinner nor sanctify the saint, while explaining the rightful place, content, and purposes of the Mosaic Law. In addition, he exposes legalism in its various forms and fleshes it out practically for others to discern from his years of observation and experience as a pastor. I also enjoyed how Dr. Mike showed the problem of legalism historically throughout the Church Age. Unfortunately, there are many believers and churches today who would proclaim that "we are not under Law, but under grace," yet they find themselves practically in its yoke of bondage. I highly recommend this outstanding, well-written book on a subject that touches all of our lives. Galatians 5:1: *Stand fast therefore in the liberty by which Christ has made us free, and do not be entangled again with a yoke of bondage.*

> —*Dr. Dennis Rokser, Senior Pastor of Duluth Bible Church and the Grace Institute of Biblical Studies*

When it comes to biblical concepts that are widely misunderstood, there are two that stand out. The first is grace. Grace is a foundational principle the significance of which is frequently overlooked or predictably downplayed. The second is the Law. The Law, like grace, is an equally essential theme in Scripture. Yet, throughout church history, it has been the victim of such misinformation and inaccurate teaching that the mere mention of the word "law" engenders feelings of nervous uncertainty. This is unfortunate indeed, since a proper understanding of the role of the Law is vital for daily Christian living. Over the years, my friend and colleague Dr. Mike Halsey has introduced untold numbers of people to a friend called "grace" through his exceptional writing ability, brilliant theological mind, and faithful teaching ministry. In *Laying*

Down the Law, he introduces us to another dear friend, "the Law." Using clever illustrations, meaningful anecdotes, and his inimitable wit, Halsey strips away layers of confusion and reminds the reader that the Law, when properly understood, is worthy of a warm embrace.

—*J.B. Hixson, Founder, Not by Works*

This book presents a good, honest look at the Old Testament Law, going beyond the Ten Commandments to examine its effect on the nation of Israel and the early Christians of New Testament times. Though exhaustive at times, it holds the reader's interest with many illustrations of things most churchgoers are very familiar with, where the OT Law is combined with the grace of the NT. Indeed, most churches have "rules of conduct" guiding the behavior of their members and especially officers and their families.

Halsey traces the thread of legalism from theology gleaned by early Church Fathers' writings, through Augustine, Aquinas, Luther, Calvin, and the Council of Trent. All is examined by scrutiny of Scripture itself. Halsey is certainly not a Calvinist and takes a careful dispensationalist approach in his examination of familiar rules in the light of OT and NT teachings and the reality of church practice

—*Rev. David J. Bauer, Director, Bible Related Ministries*

Is the church-age believer obligated to obey the Old Testament Law? Should we observe Sunday as the Christian Sabbath? What about tithing? In this short book, Halsey tackles these questions and more. *Laying Down the Law* treats the believer's relationship to the Law with thoroughness, using an abundance of illustrations to make what could have been a dry treatise into an interesting read. His conclusions are spot on. This book should be helpful for the serious believer seeking to lead a more godly life.

—*Bruce Baker, PhD, author and former pastor*

LAYING DOWN THE LAW

LAYING DOWN THE LAW
Embracing Grace

Dr. Michael D. Halsey

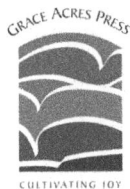

GRACE ACRES PRESS

CULTIVATING JOY

LEE'S SUMMIT, MISSOURI

Grace Acres Press
312 Greenwich St. #118
Lee's Summit, MO 64082
www.GraceAcresPress.com

Grace Acres Press also publishes books in a variety of electronic formats. Some content that appears in print may not be available in electronic books.

Scripture quotations are from the ESV® Bible (The Holy Bible, English Standard Version®), copyright © 2001 by Crossway, a publishing ministry of Good News Publishers. Used by permission. All rights reserved.

ISBN: 978-1-60265-076-3

Library of Congress Control Number: 2020943617

Printed in United States of America
25 24 23 22 21 20   01 02 03 04 05 06 07 08

Contents

Preface

The book you are holding was birthed by and for the confused, the hurting, the scared, and the ignorant, and for those torn apart by the hammer and tongs of the Mosaic Law.

On the one hand, *Laying Down the Law* came about because of people like Larry and his wife, the father and mother of a sick child. The distraught parents were toe-to-toe with a hard question: Should they buy their baby the medicine the doctor prescribed, or should they pay their tithe to the church as they'd been commanded? They couldn't do both.

I wrote it for a neighbor of mine, a young adult whose father was in the last stages of life in a hospital 25 miles away. She came to my house on Sunday, the Lord's Day. She was in agony because she was supposed to be in church that night: the elders had decreed a special meeting and had given the directive that every member had to attend. She couldn't be in both places. Time and distance prohibited it. She asked me if God would forgive her if she went to the hospital for that one last night her father would be on Earth. If she did, she would miss church. Would God be mad at her? She wanted to know.

This book is for the pastor and his wife who had to sneak away to another town to see a movie lest their church and the entire town discover their "sin."

This book is for people who are now in or grew up in a church as I did, a church in which all 2,000 members were told to put bumper stickers on our cars that proclaimed, "SUNDAYS ARE HOLY. WE BUY AND SELL ON WEEKDAYS."

Laying Down the Law is for people like the pastor's children who were forbidden to listen to secular music on the radio on Sundays and told that those who did weren't spiritual.

This book is for those who have told me that the keeping of the Ten Commandments is the God-ordained fire escape to heaven.

This book is for people who were never told of the impact of the Mosaic Law throughout history, from Mt. Sinai, from Peter's praying on a roof, from the minutes of a church council meeting in Acts 15, to those who don't know of the great mistake of the Reformation, and the impact of Moses and the Law down to our day.

This book is for those who need to "lay down the Law" and move into the freedom of grace. It's my desire that you do just that.

Dr. Michael Halsey

1

IMPACT!

The director of the Straus Center for Torah and Western Thought at Yeshiva University, Dr. Meir Y. Soloveichik, has called the Torah "God's miraculous intervention which changed the universe." He was referring to God's intervention into world history in 1445 BC in the giving of the Law to Moses on Mount Sinai.

A Torah scroll, made up of the five books of Moses, is the holiest book within Judaism. Within these five books are the 613 commands of the Mosaic Law, the sacrificial and Levitical priesthood systems, and the celebrations and festivals that united the Jews. The impact of the Law on Judaism, even today, cannot be overestimated, as we see in the following details concerning the production of a Sefer Torah (a handwritten copy):

- There are 304,805 letters in a Torah scroll.

- Each page has 42 lines.

- The Torah scroll must be written by a specially trained pious scribe called a *sofer*.

- A sofer must know more than 4,000 Judaic laws before he begins writing a Torah scroll.

- It takes about a year to write an entire Torah scroll.

- Even a single missing or misshapen letter of the 304,805 letters invalidates the entire Sefer Torah.

- The Torah used in synagogues today is written exactly

the same way the Torah was written the very first time by Moses 3,300 years ago.

- Each Torah is made of many sheets of parchment that are sewn together to make one very long scroll (about 50 football fields in length).

- The entire Torah is written by hand; each letter is inscribed and individually formed with a quill and specially prepared ink (only black ink is acceptable).

- The Torah is read at least four times a week in synagogues around the world (Chabad.org).

If we are of an economic frame of mind, we can see the impact of the Law as stated by *The New York Times* in 2012, when the paper estimated the cost of writing a Torah to be $30,000 to $100,000 (Otterman, 2012). In 2017, such a scroll cost a synagogue $31,830 to $106,101.

Dennis Prager writes:

> No document in world history so changed the world for the better as did the Ten Commandments. Western civilization—the civilization that developed universal human rights, created women's equality, ended slavery, created parliamentary democracy among other unique achievements—would not have developed without them. ... [T]hese commandments are as relevant today as when they were given over 3,000 years ago. ... [T]he Ten Commandments are all that is necessary to make a good world, a world free of tyranny and cruelty (Prager, n.d.).

Imagine for a moment a world in which there was no murder or theft. In such a world, there would be no need for armies, or police, or weapons. Men and women and children could walk anywhere, at any time of the day or night, without any fear of being killed, robbed, or assaulted. Imagine further a world in which no one coveted what belonged to their neighbor; a world in which children honored their mother and father and the family unit thrived; a world in which people obeyed the injunction not to lie. The recipe for a good world is all there in these ten sublime commandments.

The impact of what God did on that holy mountain cannot be overestimated. Its big bang in both the religious and secular worlds ranks it among the greatest events in world history.

Impact: Art

The impact of the giving of the Law has engaged the minds and talents of the greatest artists the world has ever known.

In Rome, Michelangelo's depiction of Moses in marble is the centerpiece at the tomb of Pope Julius II. There we see Moses, more than eight feet high, posed on a marble chair, between two decorated marble columns. His long beard descends to his lap and is set aside by his right hand, which also leans on the tablets of the Law. This depiction of Moses consumed the artist from 1513 to 1515. But that's not all: Michelangelo included Moses in the same pose in the Sistine Chapel.

In Berlin, Rembrandt's "Moses" is one of the most renowned paintings in the history of art. It has been the object of meticulous study for more than 300 years. The *Times of Israel* included this in an article published August 16, 2016: "According to art scholars, the Bible was a kind of personal diary for Rembrandt, filled with connections to his everyday life. At least 60 of his paintings on Biblical themes run the gamut from Old Testament figures like ... Samson and Esther, all the way to New Testament scenes depicting the life, death, and resurrection of Jesus" (Lebovic, 2016). Included in those 60 is a painting of Moses. In 1659, Rembrandt painted Moses holding high the two tablets of stone as he descended from Mount Sinai.

Art critics have noted the special qualities of Rembrandt's depiction of Moses. Richard McBee (2001) notes, "And yet Moses is not overly dramatic or stereotypically heroic." This is in striking contrast to the majestic marble image of Moses chiseled by Michelangelo. Yet, McBee says this about Rembrandt's painting:

> His torso is delineated by a soft light from the left side that also reveals the rocks directly behind him. Then the forms become unclear as the faint light shifts over his cloak and shirt until suddenly his powerful arms are illuminated in a flash of intensity. Heavy folds are outlined and a bit of massive forearm is revealed to support the two enormous black tablets. But because his hands disappear into the shadows and the material of the tablets themselves and the fact that the tablets are thin and insubstantial, it is not certain whether Moses is supporting the tablets or perhaps they are supporting him.
>
> The face of Moses returns us to certainty. It is boldly lit and directly in the center of the painting, where the light striking his forehead, nose, and cheek creates a deep furrow between his eyebrows. The very strength of Rembrandt's painting forces us to consider the interior struggle of Moses the man, who has just spent 40 days with God and must confront His people.

Rembrandt's rendering of Moses is much different than Michelangelo's. Michelangelo's Moses has massive shoulders, and the veins in his left arm appear to the awestruck viewer as swollen. His expression is dramatic, made even more so by what Lauren Mitchell Ruehring has called "probably one of the most magnificent beards in the history of art. The locks fairly pour from Moses' broad angular face and are swept across the bulk of his chest by powerful hands. The face of Moses clearly recalls images of God on the Sistine ceiling" (Ruehring, n.d.).

An oddity of the marble statue is that Michelangelo's Moses appears to have horns coming out of his head, a feature that caused it to be called "The Horned Moses." The *Rome, Italy, Travel Guide*, 2003–2016 explains the horns:

> Michelangelo's Moses is depicted with horns on his head. He, like so many artists before him, were [sic] laboring under a misconception. This is believed to be because of the mistranslation of the Hebrew Scriptures into Latin by St Jerome. Moses is actually described as having "rays of the skin of his face," which Jerome in the Vulgate had translated as "horns." The mistake in translation is possible because the word "keren" in the Hebrew language can mean either "radiated (light)" or "grew horns."

Rembrandt didn't base his depiction of Moses on a mistranslation; his Moses has no horns.

Moses and the Ten Commandments have captivated a myriad of artists, including Phillipe de Champagne (Belgium), Laurent de La Hyre (France), Claude Vignon (France), Ferdinand Bol (Netherlands), and Domenico Beccafumi (Italy). From Rome to Berlin, from Amsterdam to Belgium and into France, the greatest artistic minds and hands have been captivated by Moses and the tablets from God.

On this side of the Atlantic, the U.S. Supreme Court Building displays the Ten Commandments, three of which are carved in stone; the Ten Commandments are engraved on the lower half of two large oak doors of the entrance to the Court; there is a marble frieze in the chamber which shows Moses holding a copy of the Ten Commandments written in Hebrew; above the place where the Chief Justice sits is a banner carved in stone. On the banner are the words, "Justice, the Guardian of Liberty." Centered above the banner is Moses, seated, holding the Ten Commandments.

In the House of Lords in the English Parliament there is a water glass painting (a special technique is used to create a water glass painting: after the paint has been applied to the plaster base medium, it is coated with a solution of water, glass, and potassium silicate or sodium silicate, which provides a protective film for the paint when it dries). In 1864, John Rogers Herbert utilized this method to depict Moses bringing down the Second Tables of the Law. Herbert's work shows Moses surrounded by the Israelites camped out at the bottom of Mount Sinai awaiting his return. The huge canvas displayed here caused the room itself to be dubbed the "Moses Room."

Stephen Liddell (2015), in a written tour of the English Parliament, noted these comments,

> Morning prayers are said at the start of each day in the House of Commons. The hallways are also full of biblical paintings and scriptures [sic] as well as the various saints of England, Scotland, Wales and Ireland and above the door is a large painting of Moses receiving the laws of God in the form of the 10 Commandments.

Impact: Law

For more than 100 years, law students in Great Britain and America read Sir William Blackstone's *Commentaries on the Laws of England*. In volume 1, Blackstone wrote: "The doctrines thus delivered we call the revealed or divine law, and they are to be found only in the Holy Scriptures."

In the 1906 *Jewish Encyclopedia*, Herbert Friedenwald quotes John Adams, one of the Founding Fathers and second President of the United States:

> In spite of Bolingbroke and Voltaire, I will insist that the Hebrews have done more to civilize men than any other nation. If I were an atheist, and believed in blind eternal fate,

While running a general store in New Salem, Illinois, in 1831, Abraham Lincoln told a story which showed his high regard for Blackstone's *Commentaries*:

> One day a man who was migrating to the West drove up in front of my store with a wagon which contained his family and household plunder. He asked me if I would buy an old barrel for which he had no room in his wagon, and which he said contained nothing of special value. I did not want it, but to oblige him I bought it, and paid him, I think, half a dollar for it. Without further examination I put it away in the store and forgot all about it. Some time after, in overhauling things, I came upon the barrel, and emptying it upon the floor to see what it contained, I found at the bottom of the rubbish a complete edition of Blackstone's *Commentaries*. I began to read those famous works, and I had plenty of time; for during the long summer days, when the farmers were busy with their crops, my customers were few and far between. The more I read, the more intensely interested I became. Never in my whole life was my mind so thoroughly absorbed. I read until I devoured them (Federer, 2017).

I should still believe that fate had ordained the Jews to be the most essential instrument for civilizing nations. If I were an atheist of the other sect, who believe, or pretend to believe, that all is ordered by chance, I should believe that chance had ordered the Jews to preserve and propagate to all mankind the doctrine of a supreme, intelligent, wise, almighty Sovereign of the universe, which I believe to be the great essential principle of all morality, and consequently of all civilization.

Dr. Carl J. Richard, professor of history at the University of Louisiana at Lafayette, writes, "This is an amazing quote from John Adams because he rejected the doctrine of the Trinity and was one of the least orthodox of the Founders" (private correspondence, 2016).

In the 1940s, Judge E. J. Ruegemer, a juvenile court judge, started a campaign to post the Ten Commandments throughout America. He said he was disheartened by the growing number of youths in trouble and he believed that the Ten Commandments would give them a code of conduct. Judge Ruegemer recognized that the Mosaic Law announces an implied absolute truth: humans are accountable to a holy God.

Among the 21 historical markers and 17 monuments surrounding the Texas State capitol is a six-foot-high and three-foot-wide single block of stone inscribed with the Ten Commandments. Although the Ten Commandments are the focal point of the monument, there are other interesting inscriptions on it as well: an eagle grasping the American flag, an eye inside a pyramid, and two small tablets with what appears to be an ancient script are carved above the text of the Ten Commandments. Below the text are two Stars of David and the superimposed Greek letters chi ("ch") and rho ("r") which represent Christ.

These monuments and historical markers were erected to commemorate "the people, ideals, and events that compose Texan identity." In 1961, the Fraternal Order of Eagles, with the support of Cecil B. DeMille, donated the monolith to the Lone Star State and paid for its erection. Two state legislators presided over its dedication.

In October 2005, *The Atlantic* magazine reported that shortly after he took office as chief justice of the Alabama Supreme Court in 2001, Roy Moore commissioned and installed a granite monument of the Ten Commandments in the state supreme court building and refused to remove it. Waist high, "Roy's Rock," as it's called, is impressive; it weighs 5,280 pounds (Green, 2005).

Impact: Literature

The Pilgrim's Progress by John Bunyan is regarded as one of the most significant works of religious English literature and has been translated into more than 200 languages. As a testimony to its enduring quality, the book has never been out of print. It has been cited as the first novel written in English.

Charles Haddon Spurgeon first encountered *The Pilgrim's Progress* at age six and read it more than a hundred times throughout his life. (I discovered it in the ninth grade, later than Spurgeon did, and when I submitted it to my English teacher to be approved for a book report, Mrs. Murphy said, "I'll bet you won't finish it." I did and rendered my report.)

In his enduring allegory, Bunyan uses Mount Sinai as a threatening reminder of the condemning nature of the Mosaic Law:

> So Christian turned out of his way to go to Mr. Legality's house for help. But, behold, when he was got now hard by the hill, it seemed so high, and also the side of it that was next to the wayside did hang so much over, that Christian was afraid to venture farther, lest the hill should fall on his head; wherefore there he stood still, and knew not what to do.

Also his burden now seemed heavier to him than while he was in his way. There came also flashes of fire out of the hill, that made Christian afraid that he should be burned:

And here, therefore, he sweat and did quake for fear.

And now he began to be sorry that he had taken Mr. Worldly Wiseman's counsel. And with that he saw Evangelist coming to meet him; at the sight also of whom he began to blush for shame. So Evangelist drew nearer and nearer; and coming up to him, he looked upon him with a severe and dreadful countenance, and thus began to reason with Christian. [Cf. Exodus 19:16–18; Hebrews 12:21]

In *The Lion, the Witch, and the Wardrobe*, by C. S. Lewis, we find a reference to "The Stone Table":

The Stone Table refers to the stone tablets that Moses brought down from Mt. Sinai, according to the Bible. These tablets contain the Ten Commandments and they represent an older, stricter form of religion. In the days when the Ten Commandments were brought down from the mountain, infractions against God would be punishable by death—retribution was swift, harsh, and irrevocable. When Aslan rises from the dead, the Stone Table is shattered, signifying the end of an era...and the advent of a new...era. Aslan has defeated death by rising from the dead...(Sparknotes, n.d.).

In John Steinbeck's *The Grapes of Wrath*, some scholars see the following allusions to the account of Moses and the Ten Commandments:

The families learned what rights must be observed—the right of privacy in the tent; the right to keep the past hidden in the heart; the right to talk and listen; the right to refuse help or to accept, to offer help or to decline it...the right of the hungry to be fed; the rights of the pregnant and the sick to transcend all other rights. And the families learned what rights are monstrous and must be destroyed: the right to intrude upon privacy, the right to be noisy while the camp slept, the right of seduction or rape, the right of adultery, theft, and murder. These rights were crushed, because the little worlds could not exist for even a night with such rights alive.

Just as the Israelites learned the Ten Commandments along with the other rules and punishments for living in their community, the migrant workers too learned these rules. They learned to respect certain rights and what things were considered immoral and wrong.

Exodus also lays out punishments for wrongdoing: "And if any mischief follow, then thou shalt give life for life, eye for eye, tooth for tooth" (21:23–24). When Casey is murdered, Tom grabs the club and kills Casey's murderer in response. This is the concept of a life for a life.

Impact: Music

In 1895, Max Bruch, a German composer and conductor, wrote a two-hour oratorio called *Moses*, which begins with Moses climbing Mount Sinai to receive the Ten Commandments. Leo Botstein, a Jewish American scholar, conducted the American Symphony Orchestra in a performance of Bruch's Moses at Carnegie Hall about one hundred years later.

In 1932, Arnold Schoenberg wrote what scholars consider his ultimate triumph, *Moses und Aaron*, an unfinished opera whose theme is the Second Commandment,

> I am the Lord thy God, which have brought thee out of the land of Egypt, out of bondage. Thou shalt have no other gods beside me. You shall not make for yourself any graven image,

or any likeness of what is in heaven above, nor of what is on the earth beneath, nor of what is in the water under the earth: Thou shalt not, nor serve them.

Because of the rise of the Nazis in the 1930s, Schoenberg fled Germany, arriving in the United States in 1934. By 1938, the Nazis had labeled his works "degenerate music" because he was Jewish and the theme of his opera concerned the Jews. He found a haven of freedom in America, where he taught at both the University of Southern California and the University of California, Los Angeles. Each school named a music building on its campus "Schoenberg Hall."

Impact: Motion Pictures and Television

No survey of the impact of Moses and the Ten Commandments would be complete without noting two major motion pictures, both titled *The Ten Commandments* and both directed by Cecil B. DeMille.

For the 1923 version, DeMille built the largest set in motion picture history. When filming was completed, DeMille ordered that the entire edifice be dismantled … and secretly buried. It remained where he buried it, forgotten for the next 60 years, dubbed "The Lost City of Cecil B. DeMille." He left a cryptic clue in his autobiography concerning its location and a group of determined fans used it to locate the remains of The Lost City.

In 1956, DeMille directed the remake with Charlton Heston as Moses and Yul Brynner as Rameses, the Pharaoh of Egypt. So strong was Heston's performance that whenever those who saw it heard the biblical account of Moses, their visualization of Moses was Charlton Heston. DeMille chose Heston for the role because the actor looked like Michelangelo's Moses. To promote the film, DeMille had public displays and monuments of the Ten Commandments erected around the country. Known as "decalogues," most of them were placed in, on, or near government buildings.

As an indicator of the widespread popularity of Moses, *The Ten Commandments*, produced at a then-massive cost of $13 million (equivalent to $117,112,537 in 2017) went on to become Paramount's second highest-grossing movie to that time. For years it ranked second only to *Gone with the Wind* as the most successful film in Hollywood history. Every year since 1973, ABC TV has aired the film on Easter. In 1999, for some reason, ABC chose not to run it — and received numerous irate phone calls from people accustomed to watching the movie at that time of the year (Phillips, 2016).

However, the most important aspect of DeMille's movie is what he told hushed theater audiences before the movie began. In every theater, the audiences saw Cecil B. DeMille come from behind a curtain and heard him give a short but impressive speech in which he revealed the theme and reason for the movie:

> The theme of this picture is whether man ought to be ruled by God's law [emphasis added] or whether by the whims of a dictator like Rameses.
>
> Are men the property of the state or are they free souls under God? This same battle continues throughout the world today. Our intention was not to create a story, but to be worthy of *the divinely inspired story* [emphasis added] created 3,000 years ago. The story takes 3 hours and 39 minutes to unfold. There will be an intermission. Thank you for your attention.

Movies and television can't seem to get enough of this biblical story as shown in these examples:

- In 2016, Ridley Scott directed *Exodus: Gods and Kings*, based on the story of the Pharaoh, Moses, the Exodus from

Egypt, the parting of the Red Sea, the golden calf, and the giving of the Ten Commandments.

- *Moses, the Lawgiver*, broadcast in 1973 and 1974, was a six-hour British television miniseries starring Burt Lancaster in the title role.

- In 1998, *Prince of Egypt*, a musical adaptation of the book of Exodus, made its debut. It follows the life of Moses from being a prince of Egypt to his ultimate destiny in leading the children of Israel out of Egypt.

It is, indeed, a compelling and dramatic story that continues to grip the hearts and minds of young and old.

Impact: A Special Day

Today, Jews around the world celebrate Shavuot, also called the "Feast of Weeks" and the "Holiday of First Fruits," a time commemorating the harvest season and the giving of the Ten Commandments to Israel gathered around Mount Sinai. Its more modern roots go back to the time after the destruction of the Temple in 70 AD. Shavuot is one of the three times a year the Ten Commandments are read in synagogues. "Some communities traditionally stand during the reading of the Ten Commandments, although many authorities, including Maimonides, oppose this, as it appears to give the Ten Commandments greater weight than the rest of the commandments" (Shahar, 2015).

During Shavuot, many Jews commemorate the day by spending the entire night studying the Torah, either in their synagogues or in their homes. They don't limit themselves to the Torah, also studying other Old Testament books and portions of the Talmud (a huge collection of doctrines and laws compiled and written before the eighth century AD by ancient Jewish teachers). During this special day, many Jews join in chanting the Ten Commandments.

Some will read the book of Ruth because it takes place during the harvest season and because the conversion of Ruth, a gentile, is thought to reflect the nation's acceptance of the Law.

Jewish tradition teaches that King David (Ruth's great-grandson) was born and died on Shavuot, which is known to Christians as the Day of Pentecost, the day on which Peter preached his famous sermon in Acts 2, a sermon in which, interestingly enough, he made reference to David's death, tomb, and prophecy predicting the resurrection of the Messiah (Acts 2:29–31).

For the special day of Shavuot, Jews decorate their synagogues and homes with roses or aromatic spices; and, as all holidays include food, according to tradition, they eat dairy products such as cheese and cheesecake, and drink milk. No one knows where this custom originated, but some think it's related to the Song of Solomon, a line of which says, "Honey and milk are under your tongue." Many believe that this text is comparing the Torah to the sweetness of milk and honey (thus demonstrating that the Song of Solomon is one of the two books most allegorized in the Bible). In some European cities, Jewish children are introduced to a study of the Torah on Shavuot and given honey cakes with texts from the Torah written on them.

Summary

A full discussion of the impact of the Mosaic Law on world and church history would take a multi-volume set of books. A single chapter must inevitably be regarded as inadequate, but it's hoped that the information in this chapter has given readers an appreciation for the historic drama that transpired on Mount Sinai more than 3,000 years ago. In countries all over the world, the account of Moses and the Law is told, sung, painted, sculpted, argued about, celebrated, inscribed in literature, filmed, and enshrined in statutes, ordinances, and laws.

What is this Law, a thing the Apostle Paul called "holy, just, and good" and "a ministry of death," and which Peter described as a "yoke which neither our fathers nor we have been able to bear" (Acts 15:10)?

2
Laying Down the Law

The Israelites, fresh out of Egypt and flush with freedom, arrive at the base of Mount Sinai on the first day of the month Sivan (May–June). As Moses, Aaron, Miriam, Joshua, and the people look at the mountain, they see a barren peak that is, at the time, just another mountain in the region—but this mountain will become the most famous mountain in world history. The Jewish historian Flavius Josephus (37 AD–ca. 100 AD) writes about "mount Sinai, which is the highest of all the mountains that are in that country, and is not only very difficult to be ascended by men, on account of its vast altitude, but because of the sharpness of its precipices also."

To receive the Law by which God will reveal to Israel His awesome holiness and righteousness as well as their sinfulness, the redeemed nation, according to divine instruction, begins to prepare for what God is about to do, something unique in world history. A new era is about to begin.

A new era is about to begin.

The people consecrate themselves; they wash their clothes; Moses sets up God-appointed barricades to keep the people back from Mount Sinai. The night before God is to descend upon the mountain, they abstain from sexual relations.

When the day arrives, it is a dramatic scene, and the intent of the phenomena was not lost on the people: they shudder. They hear thunder, they see flashes of lightning and a thick cloud descending on the mountain. In addition to the thunder, they hear "a very loud trumpet," calling them to assemble. They see something they'd never seen before: the mountain is "all in smoke ascending like the smoke of a furnace."

They feel an earthquake that shakes the mountain. God calls Moses to ascend Mount Sinai. This ascent takes three hours, but perhaps longer because Moses can't use the 4,000 steps built for pilgrims today to climb via "The Path of Moses." Moses makes the climb and descent three times. It is one of the most dramatic days in Israel's history. Mount Sinai becomes one of the four holy mountains in biblical history: Mount Ararat (Noah's Ark), Mount Moriah (Abraham's sacrifice of Isaac), and Mount Zion (Solomon's Temple).

Let's Define

Socrates is said to have opined: "The beginning of wisdom is the definition of terms." Definitions are important because they enable us to have a common understanding of a word or subject; they allow us to be on the same page.

Let's begin with the definition: The Mosaic Law was the temporary rule of life for the Old Testament Israelite believer, given by God through Moses, which governed all phases of Jewish life.

The Law reigned over Israel for 1,500 years, beginning at Mount Sinai and ending with the death of Christ (Romans 10:4). There was no codified Mosaic Law for Adam, Noah, or Abraham. Adam, Noah, and Abraham lived under various rules established by God (Genesis 3:17–19, Genesis 9:1–7, and Genesis 26:5, respectively). Whatever rules existed from Adam to Abraham, before Moses received the Law on Mount Sinai, those rules were not the Mosaic Law.

> *The Mosaic Law was the temporary rule of life for the Old Testament Israelite believer.*

I once taught an 18-week Bible class in a verse-by-verse study of the book of Galatians, and in the course of those weeks I talked a great deal about the Mosaic Law. On the last night of our sessions, a lady who had never missed a session told me how much she'd gotten from the study.

I thanked her and told her that Galatians is important because we need to be reminded that we're not under the Law of Moses.

She got a quizzical look on her face and said, with hesitation, "Moses? Moses' Law? Mosaic Law?" Then she exclaimed, indicating that now she understood something she hadn't understood before: "*That's* what you meant! You've been talking about the Mosaic Law!"

I asked her what she thought I'd been talking about all those weeks when I referred to the Mosaic Law. She said, "I thought you were talking about a combination of all the laws in the Near East, you know, like a mosaic."

So much for my pedagogical skills! I should have listened to Socrates and defined the Mosaic Law; for 18 weeks, she was hearing one thing and I was saying another.

Definition Etymologically

The Hebrew word for "law" is *torah*. Basically, it means "instruction." The Law (Torah) was given by God; therefore, the instruction and guidance it gave to Israel carried with it absolute authority. Because a righteous and holy God exists Who has communicated to the human race, relativism is a false—and therefore an unworkable and impractical—philosophy. The Law instructed the believing Israelite morally, socially, judicially, politically, economically, and spiritually. As we will see, it is a misunderstanding of the Mosaic Law to think that it was the way of salvation for those who lived under it.

> *It is a misunderstanding of the Mosaic Law to think that it was the way of salvation for those who lived under it.*

Addressees of the Law

If anything is crystal clear in the Bible, it is this: God addressed the Law to Israel and Israel alone. Its exclusivity for Israel alone has the backing of Moses, of an anonymous psalmist, of Peter, and of Paul. Moses, addressing the Israelites, asks the rhetorical question, "[W]hat great nation is there that has statutes and judgments as righteous as this whole law which I am setting before you today?" (Answer: no other nation.) Moses, writing in the third person, said, "Now this is the law which Moses set before *the sons of Israel*; these are the testimonies and the statutes and the ordinances which Moses spoke *to the sons of Israel*, when they came out from Egypt (Deuteronomy 4:8, 44–45).

> *God addressed the Law to Israel and Israel alone.*

In Exodus 19, God says that Israel, out of all the nations, will be His treasured possession, a kingdom of priests, and a holy ("set apart") nation for Him. This is an example of God's elective grace.

Leviticus 26:46 concludes all the legislation of the Mosaic Law that began in Exodus 25, though it specifically summarizes the material in Leviticus: "These are the statutes and ordinances and laws which the LORD established *between Himself and the sons of Israel* through Moses at Mount Sinai."

An unknown-under-divine-inspiration poet wrote: "He [God] declares His words to Jacob, His statutes and His ordinances to Israel. *He has not dealt thus with any nation*; And as for His ordinances, they have not known them." Then he adds, "Praise the LORD!" (Psalm 147:19–20, emphasis added).

Peter implicitly alluded to the exclusivity of the Law in a speech he gave to an important meeting of the apostles, the elders, and the church in Jerusalem as they deliberated application of the 613 commands of the Law to gentile believers: "Now therefore why do you put God to the test by placing upon the neck of the disciples a yoke which neither *our fathers nor we* have been able to bear?" (Acts 15:10).

Paul was just as specific when, contrasting Israel with the gentile nations, he wrote: "For when *Gentiles who do not have the Law* do instinctively the things of the Law, these, *not having the Law*, are a law to themselves ..." (Romans 2:14, emphasis added).

In Romans 9:3–4, Paul strengthens the point: "For I could wish that I myself were accursed, *separated* from Christ for the sake of my brethren, my kinsmen according to the flesh, who are Israelites, to whom belongs the adoption as sons, and the glory and the covenants *and the giving of the Law* and the temple service and the promises ..." (emphasis added).

It's important to remember that God addressed the Mosaic Law to a redeemed people who three months earlier had smeared the blood of the Passover lamb

God addressed the Mosaic Law to a redeemed people.

on their doorposts so that the Angel of Jehovah would pass over them, sparing their firstborn sons. In Exodus 15, we see that Moses knew that he was leading a redeemed people into the land promised by God to Israel (cf. Exodus 15:13). In

> *We should put the Law in the category of discipleship.*

that regard, we should put the Law in the category of discipleship, not as the means of or instruction for salvation. The Law set forth the ethical life for the Old Testament Jewish believer.

On the Mount with Moses

The drama at Sinai doubles in the description of God's descent upon Mount Sinai as the Israelites hear Him call for Moses to ascend into the midst of the smoke. God tells Moses to caution the people not to cross the boundaries previously set on this ordinary mountain which is now set apart as holy. No priest and none of the people are to climb the mountain. When Moses ascends again, he's to bring Aaron, his brother, with him (Exodus 19).

When Moses returns to the people assembled at the base of the mountain, apparently God speaks the Ten Commandments to them (Exodus 20:1–17). Their reaction is one of terror; they beg Moses to be the one to speak to them from this point on because they fear dying. It's here we see the need for a mediator between God and man, the need of a priest, the need of the Temple, and the need of the sacrificial system, because humankind stands "at a distance" from a holy God (Exodus 20:21). Their response is a healthy one, a response of awe and reverence, the type of fear which the book of Proverbs says is the beginning of wisdom.

The Ten Commandments

Although Christians refer to "the Ten Commandments," the commands that form the basis of the covenant are simply referred to as "the Ten Words" in the Hebrew (Exodus 34:28; Deuteronomy

4:13, 10:4). This isn't a pedantic distinction; there's a reason to note its importance.

In Genesis we learn that Creation hangs on the power of the word of God. In the book immediately following Genesis is the forging of Israel into a nation. The Mosaic Law is her national constitution, and the Ten Words are the heart and soul of the Law. The Ten Words create the nation. Like the creation, Israel as a nation hangs upon the Ten Words for its very being. This motif of God's powerful Word is carried all the way to the end of the Bible, where we learn that it will be God's Word that will destroy the antiChrist and later create the New Heaven and the New Earth (2 Thessalonians 2:8; Revelation 21).

In a book about the laying down of the Law, we would be remiss if we didn't enumerate the Ten Commandments with some explanation and commentary:

1. YOU SHALL HAVE NO OTHER GODS BEFORE ME

Does this mean that there are other gods, but that Jehovah is to have the first priority among the many? To say it another way, was Israel to acknowledge the truth of the existence of many gods, but worship only Jehovah? Or does this command establish a strict and absolute monotheism in a world glutted with polytheism?

The Bible answers that question in Deuteronomy 4:39, 32:17–21. Those texts say unequivocally that there is "none other" god in the heavens above or the earth below, and note that to bow down to an idol is to worship demons. This command strikes at the core of human nature because, as Calvin pointed out, the human heart is an idol factory. Our idols form a long list, including the worship of our own fallen, limited, and flawed unaided logic; worship may also include our families, a guru, money, various superstitions

There are no other gods!

that control our lives, animals, and even Satan himself. The culmination of idol worship will be during the Great Tribulation when the antiChrist sits in the Temple, proclaiming himself to be God (2 Thessalonians 2:4). The first command is an absolute declaration: There are no other gods!

This command demonstrates that the Mosaic Law is not a model for government in gentile nations because in Israel there was no freedom of worship: Israel was a theocracy. The penalty for breaking the first commandment was capital punishment (Exodus 22:20).

2. YOU SHALL NOT MAKE FOR YOURSELF AN IDOL, OR ANY LIKENESS OF WHAT IS IN HEAVEN ABOVE OR ON THE EARTH BENEATH OR IN THE WATER UNDER THE EARTH

In the ancient Near East and continuing on down into Babylon, Greece, and Rome, idols were everywhere. Paul went to Athens and Luke reported that he judged the city to be full of them. Ancient cities had their temples to many gods and goddesses; various families had their miniature idols to whom they prayed every day for good crops and good luck. The Second Commandment proclaimed that the Israelites were not to be influenced by the polytheistic world around them as the centuries went on and their locations changed because of captivity.

In 63 BC, the Roman general Pompey conquered Jerusalem and became most interested in its Temple, particularly the Holy of Holies. The Jews vigorously begged their conqueror not to enter the premises, because the presence of a gentile would desecrate the holiest of places in Israel. Because of their vociferous and strenuous pleadings, Pompey suspected that there might be great wealth inside, perhaps a dazzling idol of gold to represent their God. The more the Jews begged, the more the general was convinced that something of value was inside. The Roman historian Tacitus tells us that Pompey entered the Holy of Holies and was surprised to find nothing at all—indeed, nothing but a bare room in the sacred space of perhaps the most religious and zealous people in all the Mediterranean world.

But why? Why not make a representation of God? What's the harm? The reason is because it's inherently impossible to pictorially represent God. By its very nature, an idol is temporal; it will rust, decay, and be subject to both time and the elements. God is eternal; He has no beginning and no end; He is subject to none of those natural forces. He knows all things actual and all things possible; He is all powerful; He is everywhere. How does an image convey those attributes? It can't. The same thing goes for His being absolutely holy and just. He's sovereign, the number-one and sole ruler; no picture can convey those attributes.

> *It's inherently impossible to pictorially represent God.*

An idol, by its very nature, gives the human being control over God. The person who makes the idol becomes the creator and God the created one. Once God is reduced to an image, He can be transported by humans, placed in any position by humans, and even destroyed by humans. An idol trivializes and makes petty our worship of God because we have made God in our image—whereas Genesis 1 says that it's the opposite. All of the above are reasons that John writes: "Little children, guard yourselves from idols" (1 John 5:21).

3. YOU SHALL NOT TAKE THE NAME OF THE LORD YOUR GOD IN VAIN

The common idea of this commandment is that it prohibits profanity and blasphemy, but in actuality it's much broader. This command tells Israel that God's name isn't to be used in an "empty," "careless," or "profane" way. This would certainly include blasphemy, cursing God. This is another case emphasizing that the Mosaic Law was not given as a model for other nations, because Israel was a theocracy and in Israel's theocracy, a person was not to speak against God (Leviticus 24:10–16).

The Law prohibited the cursing of "a ruler of the people" (Exodus 22:28). When David was on the run from King Saul, his example regarding this command was exemplary in spite of the urging of his own men.

In more modern times, we see that, even in democratic nations, there are restrictions on speech. For example, David Irving, the discredited British historian and Nazi apologist, was sentenced to a three-year prison sentence in Vienna and banned from Austria for denying the Holocaust and the gas chambers of Auschwitz in two speeches given 17 years before the sentencing. (The Holocaust most certainly occurred. Irving was wrong. To deny it was a crime in Vienna.)

In America, we're familiar with Justice Oliver Wendell Holmes's quote about free speech: "The most stringent protection of free speech would not protect a man in falsely shouting fire in a theatre and causing a panic." But the truth is that a man can't shout *anything* in a crowded theater or he'll be expelled from the premises. By the act of purchasing his ticket, he promised to limit the content and volume of his speech.

We may be familiar with Holmes's statement, but it's a good bet that we've forgotten the fact that

> a major attempt to regulate freedom of speech occurred during World War I. In 1917, Congress passed the Federal Espionage Act. This law prohibited all false statements intending to interfere with the military forces of the country or to promote the success of its enemies. … In 1918, another law was passed by Congress forbidding any statements expressing

disrespect for the U.S. government, the Constitution, the flag, or army and navy uniforms. (From The Constitutional Rights Foundation, n.d.)

This commandment also forbids speaking of God in a way that's trivial and careless.

Corporations are conscious of their brands. They don't want their names associated with an athlete who beats his wife or fires a gun in a bar. That's why there's a morals clause in their endorsement contracts.

Companies don't want their names associated with the Communist Party, the Republican or Democratic parties, or the Ku Klux Klan. One's name is one's reputation, and companies pay their lawyers to guard that name. Violate a corporation's name, and lawsuits abound. In other words, brand is character, what the corporation stands for.

A corporation wouldn't approve a commercial that began with an actor's saying, "Here at our Nazi rally in New York City, [corporate product] is our choice." Companies don't want their names, their logos, or their products displayed at a gathering of Hell's Angels in Las Vegas. Corporations get nervous when a comedian uses their brand as the butt of a joke.

The same is true of God. His name represents and sums up His entire character and person. To use that name brings Him and His reputation into whatever the situation might be. When we associate His name with something, for something, or in some situation that's contrary to His character, we are lying and misrepresenting Him. In Psalm 139:19 ff, David recognizes the far-reaching implications of this commandment and disassociates himself vociferously from

> **His name represents and sums up His entire character and person.**

When President Kennedy was assassinated in 1963, there was an emotional outpouring of grief made concrete renaming places: Cape Canaveral became Cape Kennedy; Idlewild Airport became the John F. Kennedy International Airport just a month after the assassination; four days after his murder, the first schools renamed for him were the Kennedy Elementary School in Butte, Montana, and the John F. Kennedy Middle School on Long Island; cities and towns renamed streets, roads, and avenues in his honor. In 1964, Benjamin Franklin's image was removed from the half dollar and the Kennedy half dollar took its place. Then there were the trinkets and souvenirs — commemorative plates, glass bottle decanters, drinking glass tumblers, and people read the advertisement, "Kennedy art: glass bubble-controlled paper weights." Finally, one night on the highly rated *Tonight Show*, host Jack Paar held up an advertisement he'd found in *The New York Post* for a cheap "John F. Kennedy memorial license plate." He sharply criticized it for its bad taste, saying, "Enough is enough."

fellow Israelites who want him to join them in a plot to murder someone in the name of God.

We misuse the name of God today when we claim God's leading for some act He forbids when we know from Scripture that this is not according to the revealed will of God. This happens all the time: for example, when a girl falls in love with an unbeliever and marries him, she claims, "God put us together; it was His will," when we have a clear statement to the contrary in 1 Corinthians 7:39.

Can you think of a joke about God that Jesus or the Apostles told? I can't, and that's because doing so would be taking God's name in an empty, careless, and profane way.

What do you think about having God's or Jesus' name on bumper stickers, saying, "Honk If You Love Jesus," or "Try Jesus: if you don't like Him Satan will take you back," or the one in which Jesus' name is written in the florid style of the logo of Coca-Cola, "Enjoy Jesus Christ: Thou shalt never thirst"?

What about Christian T-shirts? There's one that has the logo of the Heinz Corporation. The bright red shirt says, "CATCH UP WITH JESUS—BLESSED FROM MY HEAD TO-MA-TOES." Then there's the T-shirt in Home Depot orange, complete with their box logo. Inside the box it says, "The Holy Spirit" and underneath the box we read, "YOU CAN DO IT HE WILL HELP." Also advertised is the bold shirt in red and black with this advice: "RUN WITH JC." One can also purchase the green, yellow, and gold shirt with the Subway Sandwich logo, only this one reads, "HISWAY," complete with arrows.

What do you think of having God's name, no matter how it's used, on a trinket, T-shirt, or bumper sticker? Bad taste? Irreverent? Blasphemous? Is it an empty, trivial, profane use of God's name?

Philippians 2:9–11 comes to mind: "For this reason also, God highly exalted Him, and bestowed on Him the name which is above every name, so that at the name of Jesus EVERY KNEE WILL BOW, of those who are in heaven and on earth and under the earth, and that every tongue will confess that Jesus Christ is Lord, to the glory of God the Father." As the psalmist wrote: "O Lord, our Lord, How majestic is Your name in all the earth!" Should we make the One whom God exalts the punchline of a joke, the theme of a T-shirt, or the subject of a bumper sticker?

4. REMEMBER THE SABBATH [SATURDAY], TO KEEP IT HOLY

This is the longest of the Ten Commandments, and later in the Bible we learn that Israel's observance of the Sabbath is the sign of the Mosaic Covenant (Exodus 31:12 17). This is the only one of the Ten Commandments not repeated in the New Testament. For those who say that Sunday is the Christian's Sabbath (a contradiction of language), we would ask, "How then can you dismiss the rules and binding regulations of the Sabbath, such as capital punishment for its violation?" A law without a consequence is no law.

There is no evidence that there was a command to keep the Sabbath prior to the Mosaic Law, and there is no New Testament command to continue its observance after the death of Christ. Nevertheless, we see traces in history of the mistaken attempt to apply this command in America. As Richard Zacks records:

> When Theodore Roosevelt was [the New York City] police commissioner, from 1895 to 1897, he tried to stop the sales of beer, wine and liquor on Sundays in [the 15,000] saloons on Manhattan Island. Men and women, who worked six days a week in that era, were not amused. New York State Sabbath laws already forbade attending sporting events or theater performances, or selling groceries, after 10 a.m. on

Sundays; the excise laws also made it illegal to sell alcohol in bars, saloons and taverns all 24 hours of the Lord's Day.

Fearless and bullheaded, the new commissioner vowed to enforce the law, both to root out bribery in the Police Department and also to reunite families on Sundays. He gave speeches envisioning hard-working men picnicking with wives and children. He anticipated a drop in drunk and disorderly arrests (then the city's highest arrest category) and a decline in Monday hospital visits. He expected that wages saved from saloons would help feed families and pay the rent. Roosevelt soon encouraged cops to shut down the bars at the stroke of midnight on Saturday (Zacks, 2012).

God gives two reasons for the institution of rest on Israel's special day of the week. In Exodus 20:11, we are told that Creation was complete on the sixth day. It was finished and nothing could be added. They were invited to enter His rest and enjoy His work. God reveals the second reason in Deuteronomy 5:15: the people of Israel must remember that they were slaves in Egypt and that God brought them out of slavery, so they should give their slaves a chance to rest as they do on the Sabbath. (The issue of slavery will be taken up later in this book.)

There are other aspects to Israel's observance: the Sabbath is a reminder to Israel that God is their sanctifier (the One who set them apart); He is their God (Ezekiel 20:12, 20). I attended a Jewish service in a synagogue. They filled the time with standing, sitting, listening, and reciting. During the highly liturgical service, the people recited over and over again references to "Queen Sabbath." I learned later that Jewish liturgy often personifies the Sabbath as a bride or a queen.

From the freedom of the Grace Dispensation, we rightly view the Sabbath laws as highly restrictive (*cf.* Exodus 35:2–3) and, as Peter said, as "a yoke," but from *Judaism 101* we learn that:

To those who observe Shabbat, it is a precious gift from G-d, a day of great joy eagerly awaited throughout the week, a time when we can set aside all of our weekday concerns and devote ourselves to higher pursuits. In Jewish literature, poetry and music, Shabbat is described as a bride or queen, as in the popular Shabbat hymn [which says], "Come, my beloved, to meet the [Sabbath] bride." It is said, "More than Israel has kept Shabbat, Shabbat has kept Israel" (Rich, 2011a).

Shabbat is the most important ritual observance in Judaism. It is the only ritual observance instituted in the Ten Commandments. It is also the most important special day, even more important than Yom Kippur (the Day of Atonement). This is clear from the fact that more opportunities for congregants to be called up to the Torah are given on Shabbat than on any other day.

Paul would disagree with the choice of "delight" to describe the Mosaic Law (unless it were used lawfully — 1 Timothy 1). He called it a "ministration of death" (2 Corinthians 3) and wrote of the guilt and condemnation it brings (Romans 3:19–20; 7:7–10, 13).

It is a mistake to think that the Sabbath, as instituted by the Law, was a day of corporate worship for the nation. On the contrary, it was a day dedicated ("set apart") to God which could be characterized as a "NO" day: there was to be no gathering of manna (Exodus 16:23 30), no traveling (Exodus 16:29), no kindling of fire (Exodus 35:3), and no gathering of wood (Numbers 15:32–36). By these prohibitions, God defined what the Law meant by "rest." By these NOs,

The individual Israelite might worship on that day, but there was no corporate worship.

we see that the day wasn't a time of total inactivity. The individual Israelite might worship on that day, but there was no corporate worship.

The synagogue services of which we read in the New Testament originated not with the Law, but during the Babylonian captivity. The references to the "holy convocation" in connection with the Sabbath didn't refer to corporate worship. Such references were for the priests only, and the places where they occurred were either in the Temple or the Tabernacle for the purpose of sacrifices. On the Sabbath, the priests could do the work of sacrificing.

5. HONOR YOUR FATHER AND YOUR MOTHER

This is the first commandment that carries a promise. The fifth commandment shows the deep concern God had for the divine institution of the family in Israel. God included this command to protect the authority structure in the family (the basic unit in Israel). From this commandment, we see the importance of the stability and healthy functioning of family, in

> *God included this command to protect the authority structure in the family.*

that rebellion against parental authority was considered a crime against the state.

When a child rebelled against his parents to the point that they were not able to deal with him any longer, they were to turn him over to the state for the administration of capital punishment. This severest of all penalties demonstrates that God considered the health and stability of the family to be more important than the life of an individual rebel within that family (Deuteronomy 21:18–21). Capital punishment for rebellion against the basic unit of society was a safeguard for the nation. However, the penalty could not be applied without a trial. The Mosaic Law also protected children, because if there was to be capital punishment, it should be carried out only by the state after a trial, not on the whim of an angry parent.

The parent represents God to the children in the family. Just as God gives life to each Israelite and is to be honored for that gift, so parents are to be honored for being God's instruments to give life to their children. This honor includes obedience, respect, and gratitude. The promise attached to the fifth commandment demonstrates once again that the Mosaic Law is exclusively for Israel and Israel only, because the promise has to do with the Promised Land, the land promised to Israel in the Abrahamic and Palestinian covenants.

However, for at least one generation now, the West has engaged in an experiment with the family. The experiment has consisted of carefully and patiently deconstructing the basic building block of the family and replacing it with an entirely new set of values. As Stephen Pollard, an English journalist, noted in 2011,

> The evidence has been clear for years that the breakdown of the traditional family, of the respect for elders, of discipline, of responsibility, of reward for hard work, of the making of one's way was having a terrible impact.

> No one can deny that we have bred feckless, lawless males who pass on to their own children the same mistakes and multiply them with each new cycle of parenting.

> Ignore the hand wringing about jobs and poverty or young people's disconnection from the rest of society … there was far worse unemployment in the Thirties and genuine grinding poverty, yet rioting was nowhere to be seen.

> What's different now? Certainly a lack of discipline and the absence of a moral compass which for many generations was embedded across society—the difference between right and wrong.

> But what lies at the top of the pyramid of causes is the destruction wrought to the family, for so long the mainstay of society and

the means by which successive generations were civilized and socialized.

There are those at work — and succeeding in that work — to tear the biblical model of a family apart by an attack on marriage. Micah Clark notes that what is striking about their effort is that they admit their ultimate goal is not "marriage equality," but instead the tearing-down of the traditional family as defined by the Bible:

> Lesbian journalist Masha Gessen admits that homosexual activists are lying about their radical political agenda. She says that they don't want to access the institution of marriage; they want to radically redefine and eventually eliminate it.

> In an interview on the radio, she said, "It's a no-brainer that [homosexual activists] should have the right to marry, but I also think equally that it's a no-brainer that the institution of marriage should not exist. ... [F]ighting for gay marriage generally involves lying about what we are going to do with marriage when we get there — because we lie that the institution of marriage is not going to change, and that is a lie. The institution of marriage is going to change, and it should change. And again, I don't think it should exist. And I don't like taking part in creating fictions about my life. That's sort of not what I had in mind when I came out thirty years ago (Clark, 2013).

As the change comes, it will open a Pandora's Box of unintended consequences.

6. YOU SHALL NOT MURDER

It is this command that gives every person the right to their own life and makes human life sacred, different from animal and plant life. But, as is always the case when a society rejects the Bible, confusion abounds.

On Saturday, May 28, 2016, at the Cincinnati Zoo, a three-year-old child fell into the enclosure of a 17-year-old, 400-pound gorilla named Harambe. For 10 to 15 terrifying minutes, the boy was alone with the adult male gorilla. Harambe grabbed the child and began dragging him from one end of the enclosure to the other. To save the boy's life, zoo officials, knowing that any tranquilizer darts would require several minutes to take effect and would agitate the animal, ordered the killing of the gorilla. When that occurred, a worldwide outrage ensued.

Facebook pages like "Justice for Harambe" began to spread, one quickly gaining 11,000 "Likes." An online petition demanding the passing of new legislation garnered 60,000 signatures. Visitors left flowers and sympathy cards at the statue of a gorilla in the zoo. Tens of thousands of people gathered around the country to demand the punishment of the child's parents for causing the "senseless murder" of the gorilla.

"I was someone, and my life mattered," read the caption under a picture of Harambe on a Facebook memorial page. Heartbroken citizens planned a candlelight vigil. Some protested outside the zoo. Some extreme commenters, reacting to the online story, suggested that the evolutionary principle of the survival of the fittest should have been put into play: the boy and the beast should have been allowed to fight it out. Really?

So, the question becomes: Does "Thou shalt not kill" apply to Harambe? Was his killing a murder, an assassination, as some called it? For those in our culture who reject the Word of God, yes, it could have been considered murder.

How about "Thou shalt not kill" in relation to warfare? During the U.S. Civil War, the Seventh Day Adventists drew up a statement giving their opposition to serving in the military based on two of the Ten Commandments, the Fourth and the Sixth. Once in the military, they would be forced to labor on Saturday (in contravention of their religious beliefs). Then, by being forced into the war, their hands would be stained with blood, thereby causing them to break the Sixth Commandment. Throughout American history, there have been "peace churches" whose members are exempted from fighting as conscientious objectors. One of the Scriptures they cite is Exodus 20:13. The 19th-century evangelist Dwight L. Moody was a pacifist.

It's unfortunate that various Bible translations, such as the King James Version, the Modern English Version, and the American Standard Version, render the word as "kill." Dr. Charles Ryrie (1966), in his succinct way, gets to the crux of the matter: "The verb ['kill'] used in this verse [Exodus 20:13] occurs 49 times in the Old Testament and in every relevant use it means 'to murder,' especially with premeditation. It is never used of animals, God, angels, or enemies in battle."

Genesis 1:26–27 is the basis of the Sixth Commandment and the basis of capital punishment for murder as stated in Genesis 9:6: God created man in His image and likeness. The life of a human being is precious.

> **The life of a human being is precious.**

7. YOU SHALL NOT COMMIT ADULTERY

The Seventh Commandment is a shield that protects marriage, family, home, and society. This command establishes the right of every person to his own home. It also differentiates a man's wife from property, as the next commandment will demonstrate.

Adultery is a serious sin because it destroys a marriage, a family, and a home, thereby damaging society, of which the home is the foundation. Speaking at the Founder's Banquet of Dallas Theological Seminary on February 23, 1968, R. G. LeTourneau said, "The family unit of society is a basic foundation. Whatever changes occur that are not built on this family unit or the sanctity of the home cannot contribute to the welfare of our society. And if we allow the family unit to be destroyed in this country, we will most certainly fall."

If the family is the foundation of society, then marriage is the foundation of the family. A thriving family has far-reaching consequences for a nation. Studies have demonstrated that in order to have a robust economy, a nation must have thriving two-parent families. One study found that the cost of family fragmentation to Virginia taxpayers is at least $750 million annually (Family Foundation, n.d.).

Marriage is the foundation of the family.

Nicholas Zill, a psychologist, and Bradford Wilcox, a professor of sociology at the University of Virginia, conducted a study on education in Florida, a state with high-performing schools but slightly below-average outcomes. Their report indicates that strong, biblical families produce children who do well in school:

> Only 66 percent of Florida children live in married-parent homes; the state ranks 37th in that metric. Why would that affect student performance? Well, we know that children, especially boys, who are raised in single-parent homes are more likely to flounder in school and to end up suspended. And Florida has a greater share of children living in unmarried families than do most states in America. [O]ne of the strongest predictors of Florida high-school graduation rates, in counties across the state, is the share of public-school families headed by married parents. When we examine county trends, we find that family structure is a better predictor of graduation rates than is family income, race, or ethnicity in counties across the state .... [G]raduation rates rise four percentage points for every ten-percentage-point rise in the percentage of Florida families headed by married couples in counties across the Sunshine State.

Wilcox summarized their research in 2016, concluding that

> educational leaders, policy reformers, and business leaders who are interested in boosting the fortunes of Florida's schools need to look beyond the classroom. In trying to tackle the Florida paradox—high-performance schools, middling student outcomes—they also need to think about how Florida's families may be putting the Sunshine State's children at a relative disadvantage. That would mean devoting more attention not only to strengthening state schools but also to strengthening Florida's families (Zill & Wilcox, 2016).

Other studies indicate that when there's an increase in the disintegration of families, government automatically expands. Politicians who desire an ever-expanding and encroaching government do not pass legislation that would protect, preserve, and promote marriages and families that meet the biblical definition. Instead, they pass laws to facilitate the destruction of marriage, calling them "no-fault divorce." Courts change the definition of *marriage*; public shaming, financial ruin, expulsion from classes, loss of employment, court-enforced re-education, and high-tech lynchings await those who display the slightest disagreement in word or deed with the new definitions of *marriage* and *family*.

Proverbs 6:32–35 sounds a warning based on this commandment:

> The one who commits adultery with a woman is lacking sense;
>
> He who would destroy himself does it.
>
> Wounds and disgrace he will find,
>
> And his reproach will not be blotted out.
>
> For jealousy enrages a man,
>
> And he will not spare in the day of vengeance.

He will not accept any ransom,

Nor will he be satisfied though you give many gifts.

The author packs a powerful punch in these verses. He first calls the adulterer a person who lacks a brain and is therefore "senseless." He's a person who destroys himself—that is, he ruins his life, and how he does that is stated in the next verse: he will find physical and social ruin. He will be assaulted by "strokes" which, according to other texts, may be from other human beings, from God, or by disease.

Under the Law, the penalty for adultery was the ultimate in "strokes": the death penalty. The adulterer's "disgrace" is intensified in the next verse to "reproach." His potential influence is gone, as are his significance and worth in the society, because adultery destroys his home. His reputation is gone and his honor is corrupted by disgrace, a reproach that will never be blotted out (Waltke, 2005; see also Waltke, 2011, 2012).

How true this is! I knew a highly gifted Bible teacher and pastor who became an adulterer. Although his sin occurred more than four decades ago, whenever I think of him, I think, "Adulterer." Time hasn't blotted out the memory of what he did to his wife, his family, and his home, not to mention to his fellow believers. He will, as all adulterers, wear the scarlet letter for the rest of his life.

The sin of adultery is further compounded because, Proverbs asks, "What can he [the adulterer] do to make up for such a sin?" A convicted thief can restore fourfold what he stole. One who killed an ox can give two in return. But what can an adulterer give in return for what he's done? The offended husband won't show any compassion to the man who attacked his hearth and home. No money can buy him off. There's no way the adulterer can satisfy the offended husband; neither money nor gifts can atone. The wronged husband will pursue justice until the full penalty of the law comes down on the adulterer.

8. YOU SHALL NOT STEAL

By this command, God establishes in the Mosaic Law a person's right to his own property and the fruits of his own labor. This command demonstrates that the wife is not the property of the husband, as is the case in some cultures. By having a command forbidding adultery and then having a command forbidding the stealing of another's property, we see that one human being is not the property of another—otherwise there would be no need for two separate commandments.

> *God establishes in the Mosaic Law a person's right to his own property and the fruits of his own labor.*

Many see the right to own private property as the one essential of a society conceived in liberty.

> "The right of property is the guardian of every other right, and to deprive the people of this, is in fact to deprive them of their liberty." (Arthur Lee)

> "… no rights can exist without the right to translate one's rights into reality, to think, to work and keep the results, which means: the right of property." (Ayn Rand)

> "Next to the right of liberty, the right of property is the most

important individual right guaranteed by the Constitution and the one which, united with that of personal liberty, has contributed more to the growth of civilization than any other institution established by the human race." (William Howard Taft)

"The system of private property is the most important guarantee of freedom, not only for those who own property, but scarcely less for those who do not." (Fredrich Hayek)

Several of the Founding Fathers appear to have agreed:

"Among the natural rights of the colonists are these: First a right to life, secondly to liberty, and thirdly to property; together with the right to defend them in the best manner they can." (Samuel Adams)

"Property is surely a right of mankind as real as liberty." (John Adams)

"The true foundation of republican government is the equal right of every citizen in his person and property and in their management." (Thomas Jefferson)

In *The Federalist Papers*, James Madison and others argued that the proposed U.S. Constitution would protect the liberty and property of the citizens from usurpations of power from the federal government. John Locke (1632–1704), an English philosopher who influenced the writings of Hamilton, Jefferson, and Madison, wrote that all men "have the right to life, liberty, and property" (Braman, n.d.). In his eyes, the main purpose of government is to protect an individual's private property.

Nevertheless, there are those who attack the concept of private property. Karl Marx and Friedrich Engels, two of the founding fathers of Communism, declared the essence of their theory, saying, "The theory of Communism may be summed up in one sentence: Abolish all private property." The differences between a Communist-controlled country and one in which the citizens enjoy the God-given right to their own property and the fruits of their labor are dramatic. There's an acid test to show the difference between a state that has abolished private property and one in which the government's main mission is to protect property: remove the border guards and see which way the traffic flows.

In 1960, B. R. Shenoy, an Indian economist, compared East Berlin (Communist-controlled) with West Berlin. He reported:

> The contrast between the two Berlins cannot miss the attention of a school child. West Berlin, though an island within East Germany, is an integral part of West German economy and shares the latter's prosperity. ...

> The main thoroughfares of West Berlin are near jammed with prosperous looking automobile traffic, the German make of cars ... being much in evidence. Buses and trams dominate the thoroughfares in East Berlin; ... One notices cars parked in front of workers' quarters in West Berlin. ... The department stores in West Berlin are cramming [sic] with wearing apparel, other personal effects, and a multiplicity of household equipment.... Nothing at all comparable is visible in East Berlin. ...

In 1989, 29 years later, if we visited Poland, a country that "benefited" from Communist rule, what would we have found? Let's visit the home of a doctor. The communist officials who had promised paradise, based on the Bolshevik Revolution of 1917 and the philosophy of Marx and Lenin (which meant the destruction of private property), set the doctor's salary at $17 per month, $3 less than the assigned average salary of the coal miners who earned $20 a month. She had no telephone, a deprivation forced upon her by the Communists. One wonders how any of the miners were to get in touch with her during a medical emergency.

After we visit with her, let's have dinner with the editor of the largest Catholic weekly in Poland. He and his wife and child live in an apartment building with no elevator. We get some healthy exercise by climbing the urine-drenched stairs to the sixth floor and entering his apartment, which we see measures 6 by 10 feet. Their child is asleep, not in a bedroom, but in a closet; we notice a mattress on the floor next to the dining table on which the parents sleep each night. Our host tells us that the waiting list for an apartment like his is 20 years.

Let's go to a store and do some shopping. Not much to choose from, but we decide to purchase a few things. When we check out, the clerk totals our bill on an abacus. (Remember, our visit is taking place in 1989.)

In the early years of the 20th century, Theodore Roosevelt disagreed with the Founders of America and appeared to agree with Karl Marx. According to Jean M. Yarbrough (2012), professor of social sciences at Bowdoin College, Roosevelt's so-called New Nationalism would have a direct effect on property rights:

> In his landmark "New Nationalism" speech, delivered at Osawatomie, Kansas, in 1910, TR explained what this meant for property rights. In contrast to the Founders, who believed that the right to property was rooted in the natural right to the fruits of one's labor, Roosevelt argued that the right to property could be justified only if it benefited the community, and the only way to benefit the community was to redistribute the wealth. TR believed that some men "possess more than they have earned," while others "have earned more than they possess." He said that the task of government was not simply to enforce the rule of law, but to bring about "social justice" through redistribution.

"Social justice" is code for redistribution of wealth through the abolition of private property. The government, in TR's view, could take from those who had and give to those who had not. He said, "Every man holds his property subject to the general right of the community to regulate its use to whatever the public welfare may require it" (Roosevelt, 1910).

On February 23, 1934, during the Great Depression, Huey Long, the governor of Louisiana, took to the air waves to give a speech announcing what became known as his "Share Our Wealth Program," through which Long called for the redistribution of wealth in America based on the Declaration of Independence and the Bible. Quoting Jefferson, Long told the listeners, "All men are created equal," and based on that statement, the governor, whose slogan was, "Every man a king," explained his idea of what Jefferson meant:

> Now, what did they mean by that? Did they mean, my friends, to say that all men are created equal and that that meant that any one man was born to inherit $10,000,000,000 and that another child was to be born to inherit nothing?

> Did that mean, my friends, that someone would come into this world without having had an opportunity, of course, to have hit one lick of work, should be born with more than it and all of its children and children's children could ever dispose of, but that another one would have to be born into a life of starvation?

> That was not the meaning of the Declaration of Independence when it said that all men are created equal or "That we hold that all men are created equal."

> Nor was it the meaning of the Declaration of Independence when it said that they held that there were certain rights that were inalienable — the right of life, liberty, and the pursuit of happiness.

45

Is that right of life, my friends, when the young children of this country are being reared into a sphere which is more owned by 12 men than by 120,000,000 people?

Is that, my friends, giving them a fair shake of the dice or anything like the inalienable right of life, liberty, and the pursuit of happiness, or anything resembling the fact that all people are created equal; when we have today in America thousands and hundreds of thousands and millions of children on the verge of starvation in a land that is overflowing with too much to eat and too much to wear?

Huey Long missed it by a mile. The Founders believed that what the government should protect was the equal right to the *opportunity* for life, liberty, and the pursuit of happiness. They did not believe it was the role of the government to try to provide an equality of *outcome* for each person.

Not stopping with perverting the Declaration of Independence, for biblical support, Long encouraged his listeners to go to the Old Testament Law of Moses and read about the Year of Jubilee. Here again, he missed it by a mile. He thought that at the Year of Jubilee (every 50 years), "all property would be scattered about and returned to the sources from which it originally came." But even a less-than-careful reading of the Law shows that the landowner in question never actually sold his property. Instead, he leased it to the "buyer," who would possess the harvests from the land rather than the land itself. At the end of 50 years, the lease was up and the harvests went back to the owner (who had never lost his land, having only sold the right to the *proceeds* of it). In Acts 5:1–4, we see Christians functioning in accord with their right to own property:

But a man named Ananias, with his wife Sapphira, sold a piece of property, and kept back *some* of the price for himself, with his wife's full knowledge, and bringing a portion of it, he laid it at the apostles' feet. But Peter said, "Ananias, why has Satan filled your heart to lie to the Holy Spirit and to keep back some of the price of the land? *While it remained unsold, did it not remain your own? And after it was sold, was it not under your control?* (emphasis added)

In regard to giving the grace way, we see the same theme reflected in 2 Corinthians 9:7: "Each one *must do* just as he has purposed in his heart, not grudgingly or under compulsion, for God loves a cheerful giver." Our money, our property, is under our control.

Although not writing on the Mosaic Law, Dr. Peter Boettke (2018) summarized the importance of the Eighth Commandment:

> Few concepts have been more important for human survival, yet maligned as unjust by intellectuals, as the concept of private property rights. Since at least the time of Aristotle, the superiority of private property over collective ownership in generating incentives to use scarce resources effectively has been recognized. It was a core idea of the Scottish Enlightenment thinkers such as David Hume and Adam Smith, as well as the American Revolutionaries such as Thomas Jefferson, James Madison, and George Washington.

9. YOU SHALL NOT BEAR FALSE WITNESS AGAINST YOUR NEIGHBOR

This commandment reflects the right of every person to their own reputation. The fabric of a nation, like the cohesion of a family, depends on telling the truth to one another. When people lie to each other, when facts are concealed, when the leaders lie to the people, cynicism begins its corrosive work in the family and the society. Trust is important in human relationships, and when that trust is destroyed, the nation suffers. When members of a family lie to one another, there can be no unity.

We see that God considers lying to be a serious sin, one that fractures family unity. In Acts 5, Ananias and Sapphira lie to their church family and lie to the Holy Spirit by saying that they are giving all of the proceeds of the sale of their land for the benefit of others, when they're actually only giving a part of it. Result: God strikes them dead.

Speaking the truth to one another is vital to the Christlike functioning of the household of God.

This occurs at the beginning of the Grace Dispensation, and God makes an example of them to show the church that speaking the truth to one another is vital to the Christlike functioning of the household of God.

Each person has a right to their reputation, but maligning, slandering, and lying damage that reputation. The examples of the destruction done by lying are legion: Joseph's brothers lie to their father, telling him his son is dead, causing the old man years and years of grief. Potiphar's wife slanders the character of Joseph and he winds up in the Egyptian prison system. Aaron lies about the origin of the golden calf, saying, "It just happened," and later dies in the wilderness, coming up short of the Promised Land. Aaron also endured the loss of two of his adult sons in a judgment from God. After Aaron made the golden calf, his life was marked by many difficulties that could be seen as God's hand upon him. David lies by trying to cover up his breaking of the Fifth Commandment and a loyal, godly man dies, while the sword (of God's discipline) never departs from David's house.

The ancient adage that words can never hurt us is a lie. Proverbs says that words do hurt, wound, and scar us, sometimes for years. We can all remember an unjust or untrue criticism shot like a missile against us, and we often continue to remember it for years and years. The wound festers; the scar, though invisible, never goes away.

To protect godly elders from slander, God put safeguards in place: no elder could be removed from office unless at least two witnesses backed up a legitimate charge. The church is not to listen to the charge of one person (1 Timothy 5:19).

The Bible tells the Christian community, "Speak the truth in love."

10. YOU SHALL NOT COVET

This is the last command at the core of the Mosaic Law, and it's one that gets inside the reader—into our thought life. It's the command to which Paul referred when he wrote: "It killed me" (Romans 7:7–11). The command concerns what a person has that's not for sale. There's no problem with admiring what a person has, but *coveting* is desiring to take (to possess for oneself) what belongs to another. The reason for this command is that unchecked covetousness leads to anger at God (instead of gratitude) and anger at one's neighbor, which, if unrestrained, leads to harming the neighbor.

Those who do not have what others have become angry at God for their circumstances and for a perceived paucity of possessions when they compare themselves to others. Left unchecked, this leads to stealing and looting when the opportunities arise. It gets worse when unrestrained: when David broke this last commandment, he ignited a firestorm. To conceal public knowledge of the breakage, he deliberately got a loyal soldier drunk. At the end of his rope, the desperate David issued secret orders to kill the soldier by ordering his general to put him on the front lines and then ordering his support group to withdraw from him, rendering him defenseless in the line of fire. Little did David know that the fire was coming for him.

When Nathan confronted David, he announced that the sword of God's discipline would never depart from David's house. The rest of his life would be downhill. Fratricide fractures his home. His son, Absalom, becomes treasonous by leading a revolt against his own father, takes his father's wives (a sign to the public as to who is now in charge), and dies violently. Upon receiving the news, David, tears flooding his paternal eyes, declares in words soaked with sadness, "O my son Absalom, my son, Absalom! Would I had died instead of you, O Absalom, my son, my son!"

David applied the multiplication table to his sin. The one who occupied the office of the king was to be an example to Israel as a keeper of the Law. Instead, King David became an example of breaking the Law wholesale! He broke at least half of the Ten Commandments: he murdered, he committed adultery, and he lied. It all started with fracturing the Tenth Commandment: he lusted after the wife of another, and such was expressly forbidden in the wording of the commandment. His payday for sin was, as all such paydays are, more than he could ever have imagined for longer than he could ever have imagined.

Another aspect of David's sin was its psychological effect on the people over whom he ruled and whom he was supposed to lead. According to Deuteronomy 17:18–20, when God instituted the monarchy in Israel, the king was to have certain spiritual responsibilities in regard to the Law:

> Now it shall come about when he sits on the throne of his kingdom, he shall write for himself a copy of this law on a scroll in the presence of the Levitical priests. It shall be with him and he shall read it all the days of his life, that he may learn to fear the LORD his God, by carefully observing all the words of this law and these statutes, that his heart may not be lifted up above his countrymen and that he may not turn aside from the commandment, to the right or the left, so that he and his sons may continue long in his kingdom in the midst of Israel.

Ranking high on a list of things that infuriate people is seeing their leaders not living by the rules with which the people themselves are supposed to live. David was to read and heed the Law "all the days of his life"; however, he who was to learn to fear the Lord God by carefully observing all the words of the Law and the statutes did not. Few admire a leader who thinks the rules don't apply to him, and that was exactly David's attitude. The "Thou shalt nots" of the Ten Commandments were for everybody else, but not the king: a belief King David demonstrated by his anger at the man who stole the lamb in the parable the prophet Nathan told him.

Politicians use humans' bent toward sin by promoting an insidious form of coveting: class warfare. The root of class warfare is coveting what the rich have. Unscrupulous politicians use covetousness to encourage the hatred of the rich by the poor and as a springboard to pass laws against the rich, thus suppressing both the rich and the poor. Politicians unashamedly call for the rich to pay their fair share, but leave "their fair share" cleverly undefined. They rally the hordes to support the euphemism *wealth redistribution*, two words used where one would do nicely: *theft*. Clever words, but they can all be distilled into one: *covetousness*.

> **The root of class warfare is coveting what the rich have.**

But That's Not All

To limit the Law to the Ten Commandments is to ignore 603 others that held sway over the private and national life of Israel. For example, there were commands concerning agriculture, telling Israel when to plant and when not to plant (Leviticus 25:3–5); what not to plant (Deuteronomy 22:9–11); what animals not to use while plowing (Deuteronomy 22:9–11); and what yarns were not to be interwoven (Leviticus 19:19; Deuteronomy 22:9–11).

Some of the commands regulated the sanitation of the nation (Deuteronomy 23:12–14); others controlled their diet and cooking (Leviticus 11; Deuteronomy 14), while still others established a building code for their homes (Deuteronomy 22:8). The Law stipulated a dress code (Deuteronomy 22:5, 12) and taxation (Exodus 30:11–16). The Mosaic Law required the children of Israel to pay three different tithes: the levitical tithe (Leviticus 27:30–32; Numbers 18:21, 24), the annual festival tithe (Deuteronomy 14:22–27), and the triannual poor tithe (Deuteronomy 14:28–29). The levitical tithe was the standard tithe. It required all Israelites to give 10 percent of their increase (crops, fruit, livestock) to the Levites.

Then there were laws governing marriage and divorce (Exodus 21:10, 34:16; Numbers 30:9; Deuteronomy 7:3, 21:10–14) as well as laws controlling sexual relations (Leviticus 18).

FOREIGN POLICY: SPIRITUALLY

In the eternal and unconditional Abrahamic Covenant, Israel was to be a blessing to the nations (Genesis 12:3). When readers come to the end of the Bible, they realize that Israel *has* been a blessing to the world; we hear those around the throne of the Lamb of God singing "a new song, saying, 'Worthy are You to take the book and to break its seals; for You were slain and purchased for God with your blood men *from every tribe and tongue and people and nation*'" (Revelation 5:9). From the Jews came the ultimate blessing, the Savior.

The Law instituted Israel's foreign policy, one that no other nation has had before or since. The Law assigned Israel a unique role, one not given to America or any gentile nation: Israel was to be "a kingdom of priests and a holy nation"

> *The Mosaic Law institutionalized the fact that Israel, called of God, was to be a blessing to the nations.*

(Exodus 19:6). In the words of Eugene Merrill (1991), "Israel was called into covenant ... to exhibit in her social, political, and religious life what it means to be a redeemed people so that she might attract all other peoples to the sovereign who created them .... ." The Mosaic Law institutionalized the fact that Israel, called of God, was to be a blessing to the nations.

Solomon recognized this role for the nation of Israel when he offered the dedicatory prayer in the Temple. He prayed that the foreigner, attracted by the magnificence of the building by God's great name, mighty hand, and outstretched arm, might come and pray toward the Temple, and by doing so, might know God's name (who He is) and fear Him (respond positively to Him), just as Israel did (2 Chronicles 6:32–33).

Merrill (1991) calls Israel and the Temple a "magnet" specifically designed to draw the nations to Israel, and cites the visit of the Queen of Sheba to see both Solomon and Jerusalem as one who was drawn by that magnet. After seeing the Temple, overwhelmed, she declared, "Blessed be the LORD your God who delighted in you, setting you on His throne as king for the LORD your God; because your God loved Israel establishing them forever, therefore He made you king over them, to do justice and righteousness" (2 Chronicles 9:8).

The queen was not alone; she was typical, because "all the kings of the earth sought an audience with Solomon to hear the wisdom God had put in his heart" (2 Chronicles 9:23). The magnet drew the curious. And to paraphrase Julius Caesar, the curious came, they saw, they praised the God of Israel.

Israel's foreign policy spiritually was to be a light to the nations. Their being a light would come from their being a nation of priests and a set-apart nation. When Israel was at worship, she best modeled the dominion of God over all aspects of human life. Without such worship, Israel was not the model God had called it to be. This was one of the reasons the Temple was so important to Israel and God's purpose for Israel among the nations.

We see in all of this a major mandate difference between Israel and the church. God's purpose for Israel in regard to the rest of the world was to be both a light and a magnet to draw people to it; the mandate for the church is "go into all the world."

FOREIGN POLICY: PHYSICALLY

In 1904, Mark Twain wrote in his notebook, "God, so atrocious in the Old Testament, so attractive in the New — the Jekyll and Hyde of sacred romance." By this description, the author of what's considered the greatest American novel, *Huckleberry Finn*, was, at least in part, referring to the foreign policy of Israel toward the Canaanites.

Atheist Richard Dawkins, following in the train of Twain, but being more graphic, writes this odd statement: "The God of the Old Testament is arguably the most unpleasant character in all fiction: jealous and proud of it; a petty, unjust, unforgiving control-freak; a vindictive, bloodthirsty, ethnic cleanser; a misogynistic, homophobic, racist, infanticidal, genocidal, filicidal, pestilential, megalomaniacal, sadomasochistic, capriciously malevolent bully" (n.d.). It's an odd sentence because the author is a moral relativist, yet he's writing his condemnation as if there's an objective absolute standard of right and wrong by which he judges God. He has to import the basis of absolutes — God — in order to condemn the God whom he denies!

Nevertheless, irony and inconsistency aside, God's commands in the Law regarding Israel's foreign policy have caused difficulty. However, that difficulty arises only if we ignore the rest of the story: that is, all of the Bible's directives regarding Israel's foreign policy in relation to the nations and to the Canaanite city-states in particular.

First, we should never read the directives to kill the Canaanites as if God enjoyed giving the instructions or that Israel relished obeying them. That would be reading into the text an emotion that isn't there. We see that God did not enjoy such commands when we read Genesis 6:5–8:

> Then the LORD saw that the wickedness of man was great on the earth, and that every intent of the thoughts of his heart was only evil continually. The LORD was sorry that He had made man on the earth, and *He was grieved in His heart.* The LORD said, "I will blot out man whom I have created from the face of the land, from man to animals to creeping things and to birds of the sky; for I am sorry that I have made them." But Noah found favor in the eyes of the LORD.

It is important to note that when any member of the human race steps into eternity not having trusted Christ alone, God weeps. In Ezekiel 18:23, 18:32, and 33:11, God declares that He does not delight in the death of sinners; His preference was that the Canaanites repent, but after giving them a long, long grace period of 400 years, they refused to do so and resisted the invasion of Israel, even when they knew that the presence of the living God was with the Jews, as had been demonstrated from Egypt to Jericho over a period of 40 years (Joshua 2:9–11; 5:1; 9:9–10).

When any member of the human race steps into eternity not having trusted Christ alone, God weeps.

We know that Israel had no desire for the wholesale killing of the Canaanites, because, after getting a foothold in the land, they found coexistence more cozy than killing. Instead of marching on, they fraternized with their enemy and God's. This lasted until the Angel of Jehovah appeared and said, "And as for you, you shall make no covenant with the inhabitants of this land; you shall tear down their altars. But you have not obeyed Me; what is this you have done? Therefore I also said, 'I will not drive them out before you; but they will become *as thorns* in your sides and their gods will be a snare to you'" (Judges 2:2–3).

Second, what Mark Twain and others do not take into account, either deliberately or out of ignorance, is that God did not order the extermination of all nations that Israel might encounter. To the contrary, the Law specified, "When you approach a city to fight against it, you shall offer it terms of peace. If it agrees to make peace with you and opens to you, then all the people who are found in it shall become your forced labor and shall serve you" (Deuteronomy 20:10–11).

If the city refused the peace terms, Israel was to lay siege to it, destroy the males, preserve the women and children alive, and take the spoils of the city. This was to be the policy regarding the cities that were far from Israel.

Third, also overlooked is the fact that the predominant theme of the Law was the expulsion, not the annihilation, of the Canaanites. In addition to repentance, the Canaanites in the cities marked for destruction could always flee their hometown, thus dispossessing them of it. Deuteronomy 12:29–30 summarizes this alternative:

> When the LORD your God cuts off before you the nations which you are going in to dispossess, and you dispossess them and dwell in their land, beware that you are not ensnared to follow them, after they are destroyed before you, and that you do not inquire after their gods, saying, 'How do these nations serve their gods, that I also may do likewise?'

Fourth, the Law specified that Israel was not to attack the Moabites (Deuteronomy 2:9), the Ammonites (Deuteronomy 2:19), or the descendants of Esau (Deuteronomy 2:4–5). There were exceptions to the killing of those in the land, but these too are overlooked by the overzealous critics rushing headlong to judgment in order to find a chink in the biblical armor of infallibility.

Fifth, it is wrong to define these directives as genocide. Genocide is "the deliberate and systematic destruction of a racial, political, or cultural group" (*Merriam-Webster*, 2003). The order to destroy the Canaanites was not based on their race or politics, but on their morals. The Bible's revelation is that the one true God is a God of holiness, righteousness, and justice. As such, the destruction of the Canaanites stands in the historical context of the Flood and the overthrow of Sodom and Gomorrah.

To use Alfred Lord Tennyson's line about nature and apply it to the Canaanite culture, we would say it was "red in tooth and claw." Their culture was shot through with child sacrifice demanded by alleged deities who were barbaric, licentious degenerates. Unger (1950) summarizes the Canaanite pantheon: "The outstanding characteristic of the deities worshipped in Canaan is that they possessed no moral character whatever." No pagan religion in the Ancient Near East had a more brutal mythology than did the Canaanites. When Israel arrived at the threshold of the land, the Canaanites, imitating their gods and goddesses, were at their nadir.

Sixth, there could be no compromise between Israel and the Canaanites. On the one hand was Baal, a cruel and licentious degenerate; on the other was Jehovah, the one true God, righteous, holy, and just. There could be no compromise with the people who worshipped this false god. Therefore, God gave the command to kill the men, women, and children. Israel could not afford to leave alive a generation of mothers in the land to raise their children in smoldering hatred of Israel and Israel's God. To do so would give Israel no rest and peace.

We have evidence of just such a phenomenon as our modern world confronts terrorism from the unlikeliest of enemies: children. We have seen how children as young as seven years old are being turned into human bombs, with devastating effect. CBS News gave the following report, in a segment called "Child Suicide Bombers," which aired on March 17, 2015:

> On the battlefield, suicide bombers have become one of its [ISIS's] most effective weapons. They are like modern kamikazes and many of the bombers are children. It is difficult to know how many children have been trained in Iraq and Syria, but there have been reports the number in recent months is in the hundreds.

It's a tactic perfected by the Taliban and other terrorist networks that systematically recruit and train child suicide bombers in Afghanistan and Pakistan ("The Truth About..., n.d.).

The Canaanite women and children, if they were allowed to live, wouldn't be converted to respect Israel and love Jehovah. (In fact, we know that the reverse happened: Israel let some of the Canaanites remain and the Canaanites converted them!) Instead, if the mothers had been spared, they would have devoted their lives to indoctrinating the coming generations in hatred and vengeance. This too is part of our modern world.

The Palestinians. For generations, Palestinians have been indoctrinating their children to want to murder Jews. The basic themes of this indoctrination are:

- Jews are depraved by nature and don't deserve to live.

- Jews are occupying Palestinian land (while denying that Jews were on the disputed land for more than 3,000 years, 1,600 years before the emergence of Islam).

- Children who murder Jews earn a fast-track to a prominent place in paradise, especially if they die in the process.

Palestinian child indoctrination occurs mostly through official channels that are paid for and controlled by the Palestinian Authority in their schools, their official TV, radio, and Internet entities, and in their mosques.

The Germans. On June 28, 1919, the Treaty of Versailles officially ended World War I. That document created a generation of German fathers and mothers who lived in a perpetual white-hot heat of anger against their wartime enemies because of the humiliating provisions of the treaty, which intensified the humiliation of defeat. The seeds of World War II were planted in the words of that agreement. When Hitler arrived on the German stage, the people were prepared to listen and to follow him to get revenge because of what had been done to them. As a result, Hitler led them into a war that killed millions.

In short, to allow Canaanite mothers and children to live would mean the nurturing of a generation of homegrown terrorists and a generation that would lead Israel into Baal worship.

Seventh, we would be in error to think that God's wrath at sin was biased. He is holy, righteous, and just. What is sauce for the goose is sauce for the gander. What He commanded Israel to do to the Canaanites applied to His chosen nation as well, should they sin. The Law held over Israel the threat of judgment (albeit not annihilation) if they fell into idolatry (Deuteronomy 13:12–17). And it happened. Assyria came (722 BC), Babylon came (586 BC), and eventually Rome came (70 AD), as God chose heathen nations to be the punishers of Israel.

Eighth, we live in a fallen world in which history shows that God cannot and will not allow evil to run its course completely uncontrolled. If that were to happen, it would mean worldwide violence that would destroy the human race. From time to time, God has intervened and overruled the free will of humankind (the Flood and Sodom and Gomorrah being the most famous examples). After 400 years, God overruled the free will of the Canaanites and checked their degeneracy.

Israel now has almost all of those things by which a people are united: they have a common language, a common land, and a common holy book. There are two other things that unite a nation and they are the subject of Chapter 3.

3

Unity

Carl J. Richard, in his book *Twelve Greeks and Romans Who Changed the World* (2003), cites four things necessary for national unity: a common religion, a common book, a common language, and a common sport. The Greeks worshipped the gods and goddesses on Mount Olympus; their common book was *The Iliad* and *The Odyssey*; their common language was Classical Greek; their common sport was the Olympics.

God provided Israel with the unity all nations must have: Paul specified the God-given unity of Israel in Romans 9:3–4: "For I could wish that I myself were accursed, *separated* from Christ for the sake of my brethren, my kinsmen according to the flesh, who are Israelites, to whom belongs the

> **God provided Israel with the unity all nations must have.**

adoption as sons, and the glory and the covenants and the giving of the Law and the *temple* service and the promises."

Paul points to Israel's adoption as stated in Exodus 4:22. This was a national adoption in which Israel as a nation became the son of God. It's important to note that this adoption has never been rescinded or annulled (Isaiah 63:16; Jeremiah 3:17–19; 31:9, 20).

Israel also had the privilege of "the glory," specifically, the Shechinah Glory, the visible manifestation of the presence of God (Exodus 13:20–21; 16:10; 40:34–38; et al.). This glory was their special possession.

God had given Israel "covenants," four of which were unconditional and eternal: the Abrahamic, the Palestinian, the

Davidic, and the New. The Mosaic Covenant (the Law) was neither unconditional nor eternal.

Israel also had "the service of God" ("temple" is not in the original text of Romans 9:4). This service included the priesthood and sacrificial systems along with the entire Levitical institution.

The Mosaic Law itself was a unifying factor, and remains so even today for Israel. For example, the Jewish people around the world observe "the Torah Walk" involving their common book. On several special occasions, such as the dedication of a new synagogue or the dedication of a new Torah scroll, they come together to observe the Torah Walk, in which they carry the Torah scroll(s) through the streets to the new synagogue that is to be dedicated or to an established synagogue where the Scriptures will find their new home. In both cases, there is a grand procession, complete with music, singing, and dancing. They transport the Torah under a canopy which is, in many cases, a large prayer shawl. The dedication of a new Torah scroll is traditionally celebrated as a custom that comes from the biblical account of King David's bringing the Ark of the Covenant to Jerusalem with joy, dancing, and shouts accompanied with the sound of the shofar (a ram's-horn trumpet).

The covenants contain "the promises," the God-given pledges to Israel alone. These promises deal with the land, kings, the coming King descended from David, spiritual cleansing for the nation, and other things.

Whereas Richard cites a common sport unifying a nation, God gave Israel special events during the year which brought the people together for God-ordained purposes. The Mosaic Law specified events in which all Israel was to participate.

The Day of Atonement: Leviticus 16

On the high and holy annual Day of Atonement (Yom Kippur; My Jewish Learning, n.d.), the Law prescribed duties for both priest and people. This national event was not a time of joy for Israel; it was a serious day on which they did no work. This would give them the time to humble themselves and reflect on their lives and deeds of the past year. It was a time of soul-searching and repentance. The somberness of the day is reflected in the fact that those who didn't observe the day were to be cut off from the people. That would get their attention!

The attire of the high priest on the Day of Atonement was different, so as to avoid its being taken as just another day by priest or people. Whereas his clothing was normally beautiful and embellished with golden jewelry, on the Day of Atonement, he wore clothing so simple, so plain, that even an ordinary priest was not dressed down to such an extent (Exodus 39:27–29).

The reason for this was because on regular days, the high priest occupied the highest and grandest office in Israel before men; he was to look the part. But on the Day of Atonement—the day he was to enter into the very presence of God—the high priest looked like a slave. His outfit consisted of four simple garments made of plain white linen. In God's presence, the high priest was only a servant of the Most High God, stripped of adornments.

There were unusual sacrifices on the Day of Atonement: a bull and two goats. According to the casting of lots, one goat would live and one would die. The high priest would sacrifice the bull for his sins and those of his household. His sin must be "covered" so that he might enter into the Holy of Holies. The goat chosen by lot to die would be the burnt offering for the sins of all of the people. And then came the part of the Day of Atonement that made it unique.

The other goat, the living one which was also looked upon as bearing the sins of the people, would be led far away from the nation and set free. (Tradition says that, as the goat came to the place of its release, the person leading it would turn the animal around and back it up until it fell off a cliff. In this way, the goat could not return to Israel.)

The sacrifice of the first goat speaks of atonement for sin; the second goat released in the wilderness speaks of the removal of the guilt of sin from the sinner.

What sins were covered by the Day of Atonement? God provided the sacrificial system to atone for unintentional sins, not intentional sins (cf. Leviticus 4:13, 22, 27; 5:15, 18). Willful sins could not be atoned for by these sacrifices, nor was there any sacrifice that could wipe them out (Numbers 15:27–31). The sacrificial system assumed that some sins which were not recognized as such at the time they were committed would come to the attention of the individual at a later time (Leviticus 4:13–14, 27–28; 5:2–5).

David was concerned about his unknown sins, as was every godly Israelite: so concerned that it became a matter of prayer for the great king in Psalm 19:12; 139:23–24. Moses was also concerned about his hidden faults, as reflected in Psalm 90:8.

Today

According to *Judaism 101* (Rich, 2011b), the Day of Atonement remains the most important holiday of the Jewish calendar. It is so important that even Jews who don't observe any other special day do observe that one. They do not work; they fast; they do not drink, not even water; they attend synagogue; they "afflict the soul" to atone for the sins they committed during the previous year. From their viewpoint, this affliction of the soul is a serious time because it represents their last appeal for the year to have their names to be sealed in God's books. To have their names sealed in the books, they must atone for their sins; they must make amends with those against whom they've sinned.

The Day of Atonement atones only for sins between man and God, not for sins against another person or between people. To atone for sins against another person, the repentant Jew is first to seek reconciliation with that person, righting the wrongs he committed against him, if possible. He does this before the Day of Atonement.

There are other restrictions as well. There is to be no washing or bathing, no using of cosmetics or deodorants, no wearing of leather shoes (Orthodox Jews wear canvas sneakers), and no engaging in sexual relations.

How serious is the Day of Atonement? The following account from *Sports Illustrated* (Rosengren, 2015) demonstrates its power thousands of years after its institution:

> On Oct. 7, 1965, the day after the Minnesota Twins had defeated the Los Angeles Dodgers in Game 1 of the World Series, a 28-year-old Hasidic rabbi named Moshe Feller approached the desk clerk at the St. Paul Hotel and told him he wanted to speak with Sandy Koufax, the best pitcher on the Dodger roster.

> The clerk considered the bearded man in the black hat and sidelocks before him. Like everyone else, he surely knew that Koufax had not pitched Game 1 because it fell on Yom Kippur, the Jewish Day of Atonement, and he must have figured this man was the pitcher's rabbi. He gave him the phone number to Koufax's room.

> Koufax answered. Rabbi Feller told him what he had done was remarkable, putting religion before his career, and that as a result, more people had not gone to work and more children had not gone to school to observe the holiday. He said he

wanted to present Koufax with a pair of tefillin, scrolls of Scripture worn by Jewish men during weekday prayers.

Koufax invited the rabbi up to his room on the eighth floor.

In Rabbi Feller's account, he told Koufax he was proud of him for "the greatest act of dedication to our Jewish values that had ever been done publicly" and presented him with the tefillin, which he said Koufax took out of their velvet box and handled reverently.

Rabbi Feller's story speaks to the powerful impact Koufax's decision had on American Jews, both then and now, 50 years later. "It's something that's engraved on every Jew's mind," says Rabbi Feller, now 78. "More Jews know Sandy Koufax than Abraham, Isaac and Jacob."

To the Jews without Christ, the Day of Atonement has an inherent seriousness: on that last day, they must gain inclusion in God's book for one more year. But whether it is the Jewish allegorists in Atlanta or the rabbi in Queens, no sacrifice, no ritual, no repentance, no affliction of the soul is permanent. They must repeat the ritual the next year and the year after and the year after ...; they must be resealed in God's books for each coming year. That's serious enough to miss pitching Game 1 of the World Series!

Without Christ, the good folks with whom I attended the Day of Atonement observance know nothing of the security of His finished work. To put it in Old Testament terms, they are ignorant of Deuteronomy 33:27a: "The eternal God is a dwelling place, and underneath are the *everlasting* arms."

The Passover

God instituted a command to the Jews: a directive which, if obeyed, would be their only escape from a judgment that was

At a Day of Atonement Observance

On the Day of Atonement, I attended a Jewish service. This wasn't the service of the recitation of the Hebrew prayers and the prescribed liturgy; that would come later. Rather, I attended a gathering of Jewish folks in a room in their temple during which they read from and commented on the book of Jonah (it describes the value of repentance, even if the ones repenting are the hated Ninevites who repented at the preaching of Jonah and is, therefore, what they read every year on the Day of Atonement). During the reading from a study guide, the leader included many comments from rabbinic authorities of centuries past.

I listened attentively as the comments from the attendees took the book of Jonah as an allegory; the account of the great fish is simply a "fish story." One Jewish lady said that, instead of Jonah's being in the pit of the stomach of the great fish prepared by God, Jonah was actually in a pit of depression. The class nodded in agreement, hearing the allegorical method of interpretation at work.

During the meeting, I sensed no affliction of soul, no repentance, no soul-searching on their part, but I thought perhaps that would come later, or had occurred before the meeting. However, had I attended an Orthodox Jewish observance in connection with the Day of Atonement, the event would have been drastically different. On September 26, 2009, National Public Radio gave this report:

Rabbi Shea Hecht plucks a chicken off a truck parked behind a synagogue in Queens, N.Y., and demonstrates how to swing a [live] chicken.

"You take it by the wing," says the white-haired Hecht, careful not to get the chicken's feathers or anything else on his black suit and tall black hat. "You put one wing over the other wing. See? It's very relaxed. And you swing it very softly over your head like this."

Hecht holds the bird, waves it three times above his head, and says the prayer of *Kapparot* (or *Kapparos*, depending on heritage). He prays that his sins will be transferred to the bird and he will escape the divine punishment that he deserves. The prayer is more than 1,000 years old, and countless Orthodox Jews will recite it in the days before [the Day of Atonement], which begins at sundown Sunday. Hecht says waving the chicken isn't the point of this ritual.

"The main part of the service," he says, "is handing the chicken to the slaughterer and watching the chicken being slaughtered. Because that is where you have an emotional moment, where you say, 'Oops, you know what? That could have been me.'" (Hagerty, 2009)

Another year came and I decided to attend a Day of Atonement observance at a synagogue closer to home. I phoned the synagogue and asked about the details of the special day, only to be told that I could attend, but a donation of $50 would be expected. I decided to keep my money and did not attend.

coming, a judgment like no other. The people had seen and been protected from the first nine judgments on their captors, but there would be nothing like the tenth plague: on the night of the tenth day of the month God said that He would "pass through the land of Egypt..., and [would] attack all the firstborn in the land of Egypt, both of humans and of animals, and on all the gods of Egypt... [would] execute judgment" (Exodus 12:12).

In Exodus 11:5, God gives Israel more details about what was to come: "... and all the firstborn in the land of Egypt will die, from the firstborn son of Pharaoh who sits on his throne, to the firstborn son of the slave girl who is at her hand mill, and all the firstborn of the cattle." In Psalm 135:8, we find an additional note of that night of nights: "He smote the firstborn of Egypt, both of man and beast."

To the 21st-century reader, this judgment seems harsh, but it's important to remember that God, through Moses, had previously issued demands and warnings ordering Pharaoh to release Israel from slavery. In spite of nine previously devastating plagues, Pharaoh's answer had been "No!," "No!," "No!," and "No!" again.

The Egyptians had been cruel and harsh segregationists to the Jews. They forced them to build huge monuments and imposed impossible production requirements on them, and then beat and killed them when they didn't make the quotas. Not only that, but there was also the matter of their murderous population control to thin the Jews by killing their babies. Whatever plagues God brought on the Egyptians, they were richly deserved.

There would be only one way to escape the tenth plague: the sacrifice of a perfect, one-year-old lamb whose blood was to be applied to the top of the doorframe and the two side posts (Exodus 12:22). They weren't through with the lamb at this point; there was more to be done. They were to "eat the meat the same night ... [to] eat it roasted over the fire with bread made without yeast and with bitter herbs. [They were] not [to] eat it raw or boiled in water, but [to] roast it over the fire with its head, its legs, and its entrails. ... [They were to] leave nothing until morning, but ... burn with fire whatever remains of it until morning" (Exodus 12:8 10).

One more important detail concerning the Passover lamb: "It is to be eaten in a single house; you are not to bring forth any of the flesh outside of the house, nor are you to break any bone of it" (Exodus 12:46).

The Jews, remaining inside their homes — the homes sealed and secured by the blood of the lamb — were instructed to eat in haste, dressed for travel, staff in hand.

The Passover was necessary. For the 430 years of their time in Egypt, they had become a people stained with sin. Israel needed cleansing from sin, and according to Hebrews 9:22, "[w]ithout [the] shedding of blood, there is no forgiveness."

In all this time we never once read that they built an altar to God. Instead, we learn that they had completely forgotten about the God of their fathers, so that when God once again revealed Himself to them, they had to ask God His name (*cf.* Exodus 3:13 16). Abraham circumcised Isaac to indicate that his seed was set apart unto God, but even Moses failed to circumcise his own son. The children of Israel were far from God and deeply stained with sin when God instituted the Passover ritual (Waltke, 2012). Before the people went into Egypt, Abraham's great-grandsons had forgotten the purpose for which God had chosen their great-grandfather. Genesis 38, the Peyton Place of the Old Testament, is the sordid record of their lives and degenerate legacy.

At midnight, as God had promised, the dire and dramatic consequences begin, as the Lord passes through all of Egypt, "attack[ing] all the firstborn in the land of Egypt, from the firstborn of Pharaoh who sat on his throne to the firstborn of the captive who was in the prison, and all the firstborn of the cattle. Pharaoh got up in the night, along with all his servants and all Egypt, and there was a great cry in Egypt, for there was no house in which there was not someone dead" (Exodus 12:29–30).

That night, there is high drama. We sense the silence of the families in the blood-smeared homes as the Lord passes over them. Because people of the Middle East are very expressive and audible when expressing great grief, we hear the wrenching cries and wailing of the Egyptian mothers and fathers as they lose their firstborn children, and we feel the fear that grips them as the screams of their mourning neighbors draw closer and closer to their homes and a collective chill runs through them as they begin to realize, "We're next!"

When the night is done, both Pharaoh and the Egyptians are begging the Israelites to leave. They help them load their wagons, as at last, at long last, Israel's 430 years of captivity in Egypt are over!

God knows that the human mind is fickle and forgetful. Lest they forget, God institutes a unifying celebratory and commemorative event by which Israel will always remember and annually transmit the grand old story of the Exodus.

> This day will become a memorial for you, and you will celebrate it as a festival to the Lord—you will celebrate it perpetually as a lasting ordinance. For seven days you must eat bread made without yeast. Surely on the first day you must put away yeast from your houses because anyone who eats bread made with yeast from the first day to the seventh day will be cut off from Israel. On the first day there will be a holy convocation, and on the seventh day there will be a holy convocation for you. You must do no work of any kind

on them, only what every person will eat — that alone may be prepared for you. So you will keep the Feast of Unleavened Bread, because on this very day I brought your regiments out from the land of Egypt, and so you must keep this day perpetually as a lasting ordinance.

When you enter the land that the Lord will give to you ... you must observe this ceremony. When your children ask you, "What does this ceremony mean to you?" — then you will say, "It is the sacrifice of the Lord's Passover, when he passed over the houses of the Israelites in Egypt, when he struck Egypt and delivered our households." (Exodus 12:26–27)

The Passover represents a new beginning for Israel. In view of that new start, it is their New Year's Day: "This month shall be the beginning of months for you; it is to be the first month of the year to you" (Exodus 12:2).

Today

The impact of the Passover remains after three thousand years. According to *USA Today*, "The Passover is the most celebrated of all Jewish holidays with more than 70% of Jewish Americans taking part. ... It lies at the center of Jewish belief and tradition" (Marcoe, 2016). The celebration of their last night in slavery lasts for eight days (seven days in Israel).

It is imperative that the Jews avoid leaven, which they interpret to include anything made from the five major grains (wheat, rye, barley, oats, and spelt). The observance of the holiday includes stipulations not found in the Old Testament: during the observance of the Passover, the Jews are forbidden to own leaven or derive benefit from it. They are forbidden to feed it to their pets or cattle. All leaven, including utensils used to cook it, must either be disposed of or sold to a non-Jew (they can be repurchased after the holiday). The Jews must change their pets' diets for the observance, or they must sell their pets to a gentile (like the food and utensils, the pets can be repurchased). There is an online website through which they may sell these items.

Meticulous and *tedious* describe the preparation for the observance of the Passover in modern times:

> The process of cleaning the home of all leaven in preparation for Passover is an enormous task. To do it right, [the observant Jew] must prepare for several weeks and spend several days scrubbing everything down, going over the edges of the stove and fridge with a toothpick and a Q-Tip, covering all surfaces that come in contact with food with foil or shelf-liner, etc., etc., etc. After the cleaning is completed, the morning before The Passover, a formal search of the house for leaven is undertaken, and any remaining leaven is burned. (Rich, 2011b)

The Law required a history lesson during the observance: "And if your son asks you in the future, saying, 'What are the testimonies, and the statutes, and the judgments, that the Lord our God commanded you?' You will say to your son, We were slaves to Pharaoh in Egypt; and the Lord brought us out of Egypt with a mighty hand. The Lord gave signs and wonders, great and harmful, against Egypt, against Pharaoh, and against all his household, before our eyes: And he brought us out of there to bring us in, to give us the land that he promised our fathers" (Deuteronomy 6:20–23).

Today, as part of the Passover meal, the youngest person at the table asks, "Why is this night different from all other nights?" The answers are often sung by the participants.

Because of the applied blood of the Passover lamb, we know that when Israel left Egypt, they left redeemed. That means that the Law was given to a redeemed people and therefore could not be the means of their salvation; faith in God's Word about the shed blood was.

The Feast of Tabernacles

The Feast of Tabernacles is highly regarded. In Deuteronomy 16:14, God commands the Jews to rejoice in their feast, and it is an easy thing to do because Tabernacles comes during harvest time when the reaping is complete. Funeral eulogies and fasting are forbidden for the week.

Like the Passover, the Feast of Tabernacles was one of the three observances in which all the men of Israel were commanded to gather at the place of God's choosing (Deuteronomy 16:16). This is such a popular holiday that Josephus wrote that virtually a whole city of the size and prominence of Lydda went up to Jerusalem for the celebration; only 50 people were left in the entire place.

Josephus called the Feast of Tabernacles "the holiest and greatest feast," and in similar fashion Philo and the rabbis distinguish it from all other religious celebrations. There are those who believe that the Pilgrims, who originated the Thanksgiving holiday, borrowed the idea from the Feast of Tabernacles. The Feast of Tabernacles was also called the "Feast of Booths" because it was a time of remembering Israel's living in the wilderness for 40 years after the Exodus, so it was more than merely a harvest celebration.

The feast unified the nation: all were to join in — not only the family and the rest of the household, but also "the Levite, the sojourner, the fatherless and the widow who are within your towns" (Deuteronomy 16:14). For seven days, all who were Israelite-born were to dwell in booths. They were commanded to do this so that "your generations may know that I made the people of Israel dwell in booths when I brought them out of the land of Egypt" (Leviticus 23:43).

[The harvest] was a highly appropriate season at which to remind the Israelites of the time during God which had fed and sheltered them in the wilderness, where they had no land to call their own, and where there was neither harvest nor vintage. The transition from nomadic to agricultural life had greatly enriched the meaning of the Feast of Tabernacles. The festival booths recalled Israel's long and weary wanderings in contrast with the plenty and comfort of settled possession. Yet at the same time the booths reminded them that God's people were still to regard themselves as sojourners and pilgrims, for they were but passing through the present world on their way to their heavenly home with the Lord. (Hillyer, 1970)

The Mishnah (the oral tradition of Jewish law) specifies the size and material of the booths with care — evidently to safeguard the Law. A booth of three walls and a roof was to be constructed from the intertwined boughs of living trees (no withered branches allowed), and solely for the purpose of the festival. The Mishnah allowed no branch taken from an idolatrous grove or one stolen.

All Israel was to vacate their homes during the week; they were to eat, sleep, pray, and study in the booths for seven days. There were excused absences: some pious duty, the sick and their attendants, women, slaves, and infants dependent on their mothers.

The day before the commencement of the week of celebration, thousands of pilgrims erected their booths on roofs, in courtyards, gardens, streets, and squares, giving Jerusalem a picture-postcard appearance. As the early autumn evening set in, the priests' trumpets on the Temple Mount announced the commencement of the feast.

Today

Jewish children love the Feast of Tabernacles because of the building of the booths. Just as children enjoy building forts, so they delight in the custom of the week. They will, at least, eat in the booth (this satisfies the requirement of "living" in one) and they can also sleep in the booth, sort of a campout for them.

The Feast of Weeks

The Feast of Weeks required all able-bodied Jewish males to travel to Jerusalem (Leviticus 23:15–22). It marked the end of the harvest season. It included the wave offering (Leviticus 23:11, 17): The Jews were to wave before the Lord two loaves of bread baked with yeast (leaven). This signified the completion of the harvest and the leisurely preparation of meals, as well as being a symbol of the dedication and consecration of the offerer.

The Feast of Weeks required a holy convocation, the purpose of which was the worship of Jehovah. These gatherings were special occasions for fellowship and communion between a holy God and His set-apart people. This concept is conveyed in the details that Leviticus 23 gives for the Feast of Firstfruits and the Feast of Weeks.

In the Feast of Weeks, the men were to provide the two loaves of bread for the wave offering, seven one-year-old male lambs without defect, a bull of the herd, two rams as a burnt offering, and a drink offering. They were to do no work: the priest was to wave the burnt offerings and the two loaves before the Lord.

Today

Today the Feast of Weeks celebrates two events: the bringing-in of the harvest and the giving of the Torah to Israel. The Jewish people are careful to explain that it's about the giving, not the receiving, of the Torah, because they are constantly in the process of receiving the Torah, receiving it every day. Thus, it is the giving, not the receiving, that makes this holiday significant.

It is customary to stay up the entire first night of the two-day celebration in order to study the Torah, then pray as early as possible in the morning. Because there is a connection with the harvest, it's customary to eat a dairy meal once during those two days. There are varying opinions as to why this is done. Some say they do this because it's a reminder of the promise regarding the land of Israel, one flowing with "milk and honey." According to another view, it's because their ancestors had just received the Torah (and the dietary laws therein), and didn't have both meat and dairy available.

They also read the book of Ruth, but no definitive reason is given.

The Importance of Unity

In the epistles we find an emphasis on unity within the church, a unity based on the baptism of the Holy Spirit (1 Corinthians 12:13). We read in the book of Ephesians that there is "*one* hope, *one* Lord, *one* faith, *one* baptism." Paul describes the church as being *one* body made up of both Jews and gentiles. He commands the church to "be diligent to preserve the unity of the Spirit," "to put on love which is the bond of unity" (Ephesians 4:3; Colossians 3:14). He comes down hard on divisions in the churches (1 Corinthians 1), and publicly challenges Peter, whose behavior was causing divisions within the church (Galatians 2).

In 1 Corinthians 8, Paul instructs the mature believer to restrict, rather than exercise, his liberty for the sake of the immature believer, as an act to preserve unity. James, in a blistering condemnation, writes in his epistle of the lack of unity he sees in the church. In Acts 5, we read of God's ultimate and severe discipline upon two believers who broke the unity of the early church with their lies. All of these texts combine to impress upon the reader the importance of unity.

Unity Killers
A church will lack unity if the members disagree on fundamental questions: What is the church? Is it a business or a household? If it's a business, its purpose is to make money. If it's a

business, the pastor will be a hireling, at the beck and call of the membership, those who pay his salary. If it's a business, the members will make decisions based on the biggest bang for the buck. If it's a business, there must be a CEO, committees, flow-charts, a pecking order, a hierarchy, hirings and firings, etc., etc.

In a business, a person has a specific, delineated, assigned job; he is to do that task and no other, lest he infringe on someone else's turf. In a church-as-a-business structure, a person must seek permission to serve the Lord outside his assigned task.

If a church is a household (as 1 Timothy 3:15 says it is), then there are only brothers and sisters, no employees as in a business. One can't be fired from the family; one sees a need and serves to fill it — no permission needed.

Another Question

What is the gospel? Does its content consist of faith alone in Christ alone, or does it consist of faith plus walking an aisle, giving up sin, feeling sorry for sin, vowing, promis-ing, persevering, and/or being baptized? If there's no unity on the answer to that question, then the church has an explosive Isaac/Ishmael, law/works-versus-grace conflict on its hands: a situation, as we will see, in which there is no cease-fire.

One More Question

What's the purpose of the church? Is it the Great Commission or social justice? Is it to make disciples or to go into all the world and provide clean water? The answer to this question has reper-cussions for missions, evangelism, and discipleship activities.

A Democracy?

Is the church a democracy led by 51% of the voting members, or is it led by the Holy Spirit and the Bible? Democracy kills unity. If the church is a democracy, factions, divisions, and voting blocs will constantly form within the family.

During a business meeting in one church, a woman had a melt-down. According to the authority of the bylaws, her three-year term of service (her assigned task) was over. The service that committee rendered was perfectly suited to her talents and gifts. She loved to serve the Lord in that area; it was her passion, but now, by law, she must rotate off and cease that service.

She pleaded with the other members at the meeting that she be allowed to continue her service in that capacity, and remain on that committee. But the members knew the bylaws, which dictated that she had to serve on another committee.

She pled her case again. "No," said the members. The bylaws have spoken. The woman is so upset that she begins to cry, but to no avail. She is rotated off and placed in another committee, one not nearly as suited for her as the present one.

In this case, we might ask, "Were the bylaws made for the people, or were people made for the bylaws?"

There will be secret meetings to plot political strategies for the next vote; there will be character assassinations; there will be business meetings with name-calling, hurt feelings, and tears as winners and losers are created by each vote. People will be asked to join the church to get more votes for one side or the other. Business meetings will become an ecclesiastical mob rule as 51% impose their whim of the moment on the other 49%. The back door of the church becomes a revolving door as members, sickened by such ecclesiastical monkey business, find that they can't take it anymore and make their exit to another church or quit church altogether.

Democracy fills business meetings with tension, causing dread among the members as the date and time of the next meeting draw near. But it's not only the business meetings that democracy taints with tension. *All* the meetings of the church will be filled with democracy-created anxiety as ripple effects spill over into the worship services, the Sunday school classes, and church dinners. A member on one side of an issue looks with suspicion on another member, wondering, "Can I trust him?"

If the church is a democracy, the members will write constitutions and bylaws which, once approved, supersede the Bible as the ultimate authority. Various blocs in the church will either ignore or quote these manmade documents, as it suits their purpose.

Israel was not a democracy, but sometimes they acted like one, and every time they did, it resulted in a catastrophe. A Jewish majority voted to repeal the Exodus, build an idol, and march back into slavery. The majority stoned the prophets and eventually shouted down their Messiah's claims, "We have no king but Caesar" (John 19:15).

It's in Our Bloodstream
The problem is that Americans have been taught to revere democracy like truth and justice: it's the American way.

But we've not been taught our actual history: our Founding Fathers deliberately didn't make our country a direct democracy because they had studied the past and understood its evils:

> "Remember, democracy never lasts long. It soon wastes, exhausts, and murders itself." (John Adams)

> "Democracy is two wolves and a lamb voting on what to have for lunch." (Benjamin Franklin)

> "Hence it is that such democracies have ever been spectacles of turbulence and contention; have ever been found incompatible with personal security and the rights of property, and have in general been as short in their lives as they have been violent in their deaths." (James Madison)

The invasion of democracy into the church is yet one more example in the grim and sorry history of the infiltration of the philosophy of the world into the body of Christ. Inevitably, it will tear that body asunder.

4

The Priesthood

There had been priests before—Job (Job 1:5) and Melchizedek (Genesis 14:18)—but God had never established a *nation* of priests. In Exodus 19:6, He declares a key purpose for His selection of Israel. To Israel He said, "and you shall be to me a kingdom of priests, and a holy ["set apart"] nation." In addition, within Israel itself, the tribe of Levi would be the priestly tribe that would represent Israel to God.

We see this representation of the Israelite to God in the breastplate of the high priest, as designed according to the Law. The people of Israel were forbidden by the Law to enter into the Holy Place and the Holy of Holies where the Ark of the Covenant and the Mercy Seat stood—the place of the presence of God among His people. Although the people never physically entered those special places, in another sense they did make such an entry, every one of them: through the image on the high priest's breastplate. This was not the breastplate of a warrior, but of the high priest who was wearing it for all those Israelites who were ineligible for entry into the inner sanctum of the Tabernacle.

Carl Armerding, former professor emeritus of the Bible and theology at Wheaton College, describes the scene:

> They [the people] entered it in the person of their spiritual representative, the high priest, who bore the names of the children of Israel in the breastplate of judgment upon his heart, when he went into the holy place, for a memorial before the Lord continually. Their names were engraved in those stones so that they could not be erased or blotted out. (Armerding, 1961)

Their names were also engraved in the two onyx stones that served as shoulder pieces in the ephod worn by the high priest; "six of their names on one stone, and the other six names of the rest on the other stone, according to their birth" (Exodus 28:10). The breastplate differed from the shoulder pieces in that the name of each tribe was engraved on its own separate stone.

Thus, the high priest bore the names of the 12 sons of Jacob in two places when he did his priestly tasks in the Tabernacle: over his heart on the breastplate and on the shoulder pieces of the ephod (Exodus 28:12, 29). Dr. S. Lewis Johnson (1963) comments: "All of this was designed to illustrate that his ministry as high priest was directed to the children of Israel, the covenant people, and not to the world indiscriminately. They were upon his heart as indicating the affection of God for them, and upon his shoulders, the place of strength, to illustrate his [God's] power in the support of them."

The Task of the Priest

W. H. Griffith Thomas (1996) writes, "The essential work of the priest was expressed in sacrifice and intercession, and may be summed up in the word *mediator*. Whatever the priest did outside of those two parameters had nothing to do with his office." The priest was concerned with man's getting access to God. In that very task, we see several fundamental doctrines of the Scriptures at work, beginning in Genesis 3 and weaving their way consistently through the Bible: people are separated from God because of sin and need to get to Him; humanity needs a way to be provided by which we can return to God; and that way must be provided by a mediator. The word *priest* implicitly teaches those doctrines.

The priests of Israel were continually concerned with altars and sacrifices—to the point that the three (altar, sacrifice, and priest) were inextricably intertwined: you could not have one without the other two. If there is no need of a continual altar, there is no need of a continual sacrifice; if there is no continual sacrifice, there is no need of a continual priesthood.

Israel had a privileged position and a privileged service. Moses, in addressing the nation, reminded them of that fact in Deuteronomy 4:8: "For what great nation is there that has a god so near to it as is the Lord our God whenever we call on Him? Or what great nation is there that has statutes and judgments as righteous as this whole law which I am setting before you today?" Unfortunately, Israel failed at its God-given task of mediation and Law observance.

Corruption Inside the Priesthood

Hophni and Phinehas, two priests in Israel, the sons of Eli, became worthless priests who treated the prescribed sacrifices of the Mosaic Law with contempt and engaged in sexual immorality (1 Samuel 2:12, 17, 22). God would not tolerate such a cancer within the priesthood. A messenger came to Eli and predicted that his sons would both die on the same day. This occurred when the Philistines defeated the Israelites at Aphek, captured the Ark of the Covenant, and in the process killed Hophni and his brother. When the 98-year-old Eli learned of the defeat, the capture of the Ark, and the deaths of his sons, he fell backward, broke his neck, and died.

The repercussions of the battle of Aphek continued when Eli's daughter-in-law, who was expecting a baby, heard the news. She went into labor and gave birth to a son. The women around her tried to console her concerning the loss of her husband, but she refused to be comforted, as we see in her choice of a name for her son. She named the baby *Ichabod*, meaning "the glory has departed from Israel." The name reflected the pathetic state of the priesthood: the army was defeated, the Ark of the Covenant was in enemy hands, and now (because of the deaths of Eli and his sons) this baby was the high priest of Israel (1 Samuel 4).

Eli and his sons lived during the time of the judges (1350–1051 BC). Later in Israel's history (605–562 BC), the priesthood had further devolved into a swamp of sin: "Her priests have done violence to My law and have profaned My holy things; they have made no distinction between the holy and the profane, and they have not taught the difference between the unclean and the clean; and they hide their eyes from My sabbaths, and I am profaned among them" (Ezekiel 22:26).

Of course, there was always a remnant of believers in Israel, no matter the culture; this remnant did not fail in the priestly function God gave to Israel. Jeremiah, a priest by birth and a prophet by grace, carried out his divine calling during 627–587 BC. He described the priesthood in his day: "The priests did not say, 'Where is the LORD?' And those who handle the law did not know Me ... And the priests rule on their *own* authority; And My people love it so ... " (Jeremiah 2:8; 5:31)

The priests became so enraged at Jeremiah's sermons that "when Jeremiah finished speaking all that the LORD had commanded *him* to speak to all the people, the priests and the prophets and all the people seized him, saying, "You must die! Why have you prophesied in the name of the LORD saying, 'This house will be like Shiloh and this city will be desolate, without inhabitant?'" (Jeremiah 26:7–9)

Jeremiah relates God's description of the corrosive corruption of the nation from the kings to the inhabitants of Jerusalem:

> Indeed this city has been to Me a provocation of My anger and My wrath from the day that they built it, even to this day, so that it should be removed from before My face, because of all the evil of the sons of Israel and the sons of Judah which they have done to provoke Me to anger — they, their kings, their leaders, their priests, their prophets, the men of Judah and the inhabitants of Jerusalem (Jeremiah 32:31–32).

The Big Picture

The corruption of the priests and the prophets fits into a larger picture, the one predicted at the Fall: "And I will put enmity between you and the woman, and between your seed and her seed; He shall bruise you on the head, And you shall bruise Him on the heel." With this declaration, the great conflict between God and Satan is set in motion, with Genesis 3:15 giving the reader the plot of the story the Bible will present.

The priests—the very men who were privileged and commissioned to represent men to God—became so corrupt that they failed. Those who should have been closest to God, those who should have been leading people to God, and those who should have been part of that magnet to attract the gentiles to come and see, had become idolatrous (Hosea 5, 6, 10). Behind all of this is Satan's ongoing strategy to destroy God's plan and program for His chosen nation.

When the Messiah came, satanic opposition to God's plan moved into high gear and the depraved priesthood cooperated with that satanic opposition, albeit unwittingly. The Gospels make reference to a group called the chief priests. *Matthew Henry's Commentary* (2014) says that the chief priests included "not only the high priest for the time being, and his deputy, with those who had formerly borne that office, but also the heads of the twenty-four courses [of the priesthood], as well as any other persons of peculiar eminence in the priesthood."

The Gospel of Matthew first mentions these prestigious priests in connection with the coming of the Messiah when Herod, because of the coming of the Magi, inquired about the birthplace of the Messiah. Though the chief priests ascertain the predicted location of the birth from Micah 5:2 and hear the Magi's report of the star in the East, they show no interest in making the short, five-mile trip to Bethlehem.

However, as the plot develops, the indifference of the various groups of religious leaders becomes an ever-growing hostility. (There is no neutrality: one is either for Him or against Him.) Their antagonism prompted the chief priests, the priests, the Sadducees, and the Pharisees to question His authority, to look for ways to arrest Him, to dismiss His miracles as satanic, to say His birth was an illegitimate one, to conspire to murder Lazarus, to affiliate themselves with Judas Iscariot, to confer to put Him to death, to spend 30 pieces of silver to bribe Judas, to arrest Him, to persuade the crowds to free Barabbas, to demand that Jesus be tried, to mock Him as He hung on the cross, and to request Pilate to seal His tomb.

All of this opposition and enmity came in spite of their hearing and seeing the words and miracles of the Messiah. He offered grace; they rejected it. The degeneracy of the priesthood established under the Law was complete. The priests and high priests of Israel had become those numbered with the seed of the serpent!

He offered grace; they rejected it.

Even after the Resurrection and Ascension of the Messiah, the chief priests refused to rest; their hostility continued unabated. Since they couldn't touch the now-ascended Messiah, they turned their satanically energized fury on Christ's church and His apostles. The chief priests arrested and jailed Peter and John, warning them, then ordering them not to speak or teach in the name of Jesus. This was, in effect, forbidding them to say His name. It was this group that commissioned Saul to bind over any believers he could arrest.

Dr. Allen Ross (2006) summarizes the condition of the priesthood in Jesus' day:

Spiritual leadership in the days of Jesus had certainly gone awry, and the spiritual life of the people was thrown into confusion. Of course there were a few faithful leaders around, good people who were devout, wise, learned, and capable, who were trying to minister as they understood they should do. But the greater number who occupied positions of authority had been caught up in the constant religious battles with pagan rulers and power struggles with one another. They disagreed with each other on theology, politics, ritual, and ministry. Too often they were preoccupied with their own interpretations of the Scripture to hear the truth; they became self-righteous and self-serving. Their hypocrisy and unbelief blinded them to the truth of the revelation of Jesus Christ.

Yet there was good news, as Luke reported after Jesus' ascension: "The word of God kept on spreading; and the number of the disciples continued to increase greatly in Jerusalem, and a great many of the priests were becoming obedient to the faith" (Acts 6:7). We're reminded of John's prologue, "For the Law was given through Moses; grace and truth [even to priests] were realized through Jesus Christ" (1:17).

The Yoke of Minute Detail

A yoke is a cumbersome thing. That's why Peter called the Law a yoke, adding the qualifier "that neither our fathers nor we have been able to bear" (Acts 15:10). The Law was meticulous in detail, right down to the clothing of the priest, as one entire chapter stipulates that Aaron's clothing is designed to "give him dignity and honor" (Exodus 28:2). One entire chapter, consisting of 43 specific and detailed verses, instructs "all the skilled men" as to how to make the high priest's "breastpiece, ephod, robe, tunic of checkered work, a turban and a sash" (Exodus 28:4). The Law specified its material and colors. Nor did the Law stop there: Exodus 28:42 includes instructions for the priests' undergarments as to their material (linen) and their measurements (from the waist to the thigh). The Law piled minute detail upon detail.

Then there are the highly technical blueprints for the Tabernacle, including its offerings and its furniture (the Ark of the Covenant, the altar, the table, and the lampstand). Included in the directions are "ten curtains of finely twisted linen and blue, purple, and scarlet yarn." The measurements are precise, and the proper and precise places within the Tabernacle were set for each item. The instructions for another set of curtains, these to cover the Tabernacle, decreed that they were to be made of goat hair and to contain "fifty loops along the edge of the end curtain... then fifty bronze clasps and put them in the loops to fasten the tent together" (Exodus 26). There are further instructions as to who may enter the Tabernacle and when he may enter. God instructed Israel as to the details of its transport, its contents, its materials, and its colors.

Then there was the sacrificial system and instructions concerning how the priests were to administer it. There were detailed commands concerning what kind of sacrifices, their number, and occasion. There were approved sacrifices and forbidden ones, particulars given in one list after another.

A Violation of the Instructions

The Law gave absolute and unconditional instructions for the fire in the brazen altar, but these details were treated with contempt by two priests early on. Nadab and Abihu are best known for offering "unauthorized fire" before the Lord in the Tabernacle and dying as a result. Leviticus 10:1–2 shares this sobering account, stating, "Aaron's sons Nadab and Abihu took their censers, put fire in them and added incense; and they offered unauthorized fire before the LORD, contrary to his command. So fire came out from the presence of the LORD and consumed them, and they died before the LORD."

Why did God put Nadab and Abihu to death? Leviticus 10:3 explains that Moses said to Aaron, "This is what the Lord spoke of when he said: 'Among those who approach me I will be proved holy; in the sight of all the people I will be honored.'" Houdmann emphasizes that "[t]hose who served as priests before the Lord were required to serve Him honorably. If they did not, the consequence was death. In the case of Aaron's sons, they dishonored the Lord by disobeying His command to use only fire from the brazen altar in the tabernacle. The 'unauthorized fire' they offered was taken from another source" (Houdmann, n.d.).

With regard to the Tabernacle, its priests, and its sacrifices, the Scriptures construct a yoke of performance and the details of that performance. We can summarize the entire Law system as God saying, "Do and I'll bless you. Disobey and I'll curse you." That's what Peter was talking about when he said that the Law was a yoke which "neither our fathers nor we have been able to bear" (Acts 15:10).

> *We can summarize the entire Law system as God saying, "Do and I'll bless you. Disobey and I'll curse you."*

Never Done

H. Plotz wrote, "Man may work from sun to sun, but woman's work is never done" (1996). This could be analogized to the priestly task in regard to the Old Testament priest and the system of sacrifices: the priest's work was never done. In the majestic book of Hebrews, the author emphasizes the posture of the Old Testament priest: he was ever standing; he never sat down in the sanctuary. "Day after day every priest stands and performs his religious duties; again and again he offers the same sacrifices, which can never take away sins" (Hebrews 10:11). The author's emphasis is clear about the dreary routine: "Day after day ... again and again ... the same sacrifices which can never take away sins."

We often speak of the joy of a task well done and complete, but the priests under the Law never knew such satisfaction.

The reason that the priests never knew the contentment of sin permanently forgiven was because, in their day, there was no basis for it:

> Now, in the old economy, before Jesus Christ gave Himself as the propitiation [satisfaction] and His blood as that which propitiates [satisfies], there was no permanent basis on which God could deal with a sinner. There was no basis upon which God could manifest His love toward a sinner. It was impossible for a righteous, holy, just God to look at a sinner and say, "I will forget the fact that you are dead in trespasses and sins, will forgive the debt which you owe, and I will receive you unto myself because I love you." Had God done such a thing, He would have become an unrighteous God. Between God and man the great wall of sin had come, so that man was sealed off from the presence of God. God's love alone was not sufficient basis on which to receive a sinner. (Pentecost, 1971)

Nevertheless, there was grace in the dispensation of the Law; the sacrificial system itself testifies to that. The bulls, lambs, and goats died, the sinner/offerer did not. But this grace provision was temporary, as Hebrews 10:4 says, "For it is impossible for the blood of bulls and goats to take away sins." The blood of animals had no permanency. We can visualize the Old Testament priest coming home after completing his rotation in the sanctuary, having been on his feet all day, never sitting, and knowing that he had done nothing permanent about the sins of the sinners who brought the offerings.

Because the payment for sin was not ultimately taken care of under the Law, the sacrifices brought only a temporary "passing over" of those sins, as Paul explains: "because in the forbearance and their messianic predictions (such as Genesis 3, Psalm 22, Isaiah 53, and Micah 5), but also from the Law's description of the sacrificial system. Our anticipation is rewarded when we read John the Baptist's declaration when he sees Jesus: "Behold, lamb of God who takes away the sin of the world" (John 1:29). There were 1,400 years of expectation underlying John the Baptist's joyful declaration. Over that period of time, the Jews had brought and the priests had slit the throats of tens of thousands of bulls, goats, and lambs ... and now, at long last, finally, God's own Lamb had come!

Now, at long last, finally, God's own Lamb had come!

It was this Priest—as the author of Hebrews declares, this Priest after the order of Melchizedek—who, because of His once-and-for-all sacrifice of Himself, *sat down* at the right hand of God the Father. The work was done. His sacrifice of Himself brought what the Law could not: satisfaction: "And He Himself is the propitiation [satisfaction] for our sins; and not for ours only, but also for *those of* the whole world" (1 John 2:2).

When the Lamb of God made His sacrifice of Himself, His sacrifice was so complete that He paid for every sin of every person in the world, all of those in the past and all of those to come. In regard to His payment for our sins, He would never have to say, "If only ... one more person, I could have gotten one more person, and I didn't ... I didn't."

When Jesus as our great high priest sat down at the right hand of God the Father, He did so because He had indeed paid it all. Just as He shouted from the cross, "It is finished!" There was no remaining sin to be paid for. It was done, complete.

Yet, after singing "Jesus Paid It All," those assembled often hear the pastor preaching a sermon that basically declares, "No, it's not finished." But how can he say such a thing, albeit not in exactly those words and not that blatantly?

THE IMPORTANCE OF SITTING DOWN

In 1865, Elvina Hall sits with the choir on a Sunday morning in the Monument Street Methodist Church in Baltimore. She's thinking, "The pastor's prayer is long this morning," and her mind strays from her long-praying parson and focuses on the need of salvation and the price Jesus paid for it.

Words begin to form in her head and she knows she needs a piece of paper to record them. While her pastor continues his public supplication of praying for those all around the world, she decides the flyleaf of her hymnbook will do nicely. After the service, she shows the words to the pastor.

As he reads the words, he realizes that a divinely arranged coincidence has occurred; earlier the church organist, John Grape, had written a new tune and given it to him. As he reads on, he realizes that the words and tune fit nicely.

Today, on any given Sunday, millions and millions of people unite to sing that song birthed in the Monument Street Methodist Church choir loft more than 150 years ago: "Jesus Paid It All."

But, the question is, do those millions believe it?

The preacher says that Christ's work is not finished every time he begins a sentence of invitation that says, "Believe in Jesus AND ...." It's what comes after "AND" that says, "Jesus didn't pay it all." For example, the pastor, in all seriousness, says, "Believe in Jesus AND turn from your sins"; "... AND be willing to turn from your sins"; "... AND confess your sins"; "... AND make Him Lord of your life for if He's not the Lord of all, He's not the Lord at all"; "AND keep the Ten Commandments"; "AND keep the Golden Rule"; "AND feel sorry for your sins"; "AND be baptized"; "AND walk down the aisle"; "AND live for Him"; "AND promise to live for Him ... AND confess Him publicly." (I read a tract that inserted the biggest "AND" of them all: "AND do everything the Bible says.")

Evangelists, pastors, and authors make these additions in spite of the fact that about a hundred times in the Gospel of John alone, *faith alone in Christ* (with no "ANDs") is identified as *the* condition for salvation. The most beloved and most quoted evangelistic verse in the Bible contains no "AND": "For God so loved the world that He gave His only begotten Son that whosoever *believes* in Him should not perish but have everlasting life" (John 3:16). That should be enough to establish that salvation is by faith alone in Christ alone.

So What?

What is the import of the finished work of Christ and His seating at the right hand of God the Father? Is it so important, after all? The author of Hebrews says that it is extremely important and he makes his case with precise logic. He does so by contrasting the two priesthoods, the Levitical and the Melchizedekian. Christ is declared to be a priest after the order of Melchizedek, and that fact alone proves that the Levitical priesthood was both inferior and temporary. Jesus wasn't qualified to be a priest in the order of Aaron — that is, the Levitical priesthood — because He was from the tribe of Judah (Hebrews 7:14).

In Hebrews 7:11 we read, "Now if perfection was through the Levitical priesthood (for on the basis of it the people received the Law), what further need *was there* for another priest to arise according to the order of Melchizedek, and not be designated according to the order of Aaron?" By this, the author comes to an important conclusion. It's important to note that the Hebrews author clearly says, "for on the basis of it [the Levitical priesthood] the people received the [Mosaic] Law." The priesthood established by the Aaronic order was inextricably bound up with the Law. The two were inseparable; the Law was the basis of the priesthood. "Therefore," writes the author of Hebrews, "for when the priesthood is changed, of necessity there takes place a change of law also" (7:12).

Regarding this text, Dr. Charles C. Ryrie writes: "If Christ is our High Priest, then the Law can no longer be operative and binding on us. If the law has not been done away, then neither has the levitical priesthood, and Christ is not our High Priest today" (1986). Lest believers conclude that they are therefore without any law, Paul points to the Law of Christ, as stated in Galatians 6:2: "Bear one another's burdens, and thereby fulfill the law of Christ." The law of Christ contains some new commandments, some old ones, and some revised ones. But the Mosaic Law as a binding code on the believer is gone: obsolete and irrelevant.

> **The Mosaic Law as a binding code on the believer is gone: obsolete and irrelevant.**

aspects of a work: it must be observable; it must be accomplished by physical means; and it must be done by a human being.

What about confession, confession of sin before a priest or confession of Christ as Savior, as many evangelists command us to do in order to be saved? Are those works? Yes, because they fit the definition: confession is observable, physical, and performed by a human being. It's easy to see that baptism is also a work.

As stated in chapter 4, the single book of the Gospel of John records that God justifies human beings by faith alone about one hundred times. This is not merely a foundational truth of Scripture, it is an *emphatic* foundational truth.

You'd Think That We'd Get the Point

With such a heavy weight of Scripture buttressing that foundational truth, you'd think we would get it. Yet in my discussions with many, many people inside and outside our churches, I find that too many of them think that God justifies human beings by their keeping of the Ten Commandments (action that is observable, physical, and performed by a human being; that is, work) or at least by trying to do so.

Many don't understand that the Law, including the Ten Commandments, is a condemnatory document with a serious deficiency: it has yet to save anyone eternally from the wrath of God. Paul states this with crystal clarity in Romans 3:19–21, 4:1–16, and Galatians 3:10–12: no one ever was or will be justified by the Law. In Galatians 3:12 Paul quoted the same verse (Leviticus 18:5) that he referred to in Romans 10:5. The point he made in both contexts is that, because everyone sins and falls short of God's standard, there is no one who is righteous as a result of trying to keep the Law (Galatians 3:10; *cf.* James 2:10).

No one ever was or will be justified by the Law.

5

The Law, Lawfully

But we know that the Law is good, if one uses it lawfully (1 Timothy 1:8).

There is a foundational truth of Scripture which must guide all our thinking. Hal Harless, the director of Calvary Chapel Bible College, states it concisely: "God justifies human beings by grace alone through faith alone in Jesus Christ alone and not by works. This was the consistent teaching of Jesus (John 3:14–18, 36; 5:24; 6:28–29, 40; 11:25–27), Paul (Rom. 3:21–22; 4:5; Eph. 2:8–10), and the other Apostles (Acts 10:43; 15:7–11; 1 John 5:11). To depart from this principle is to depart from the orthodox Christian faith" (2003).

The Bible states this foundational truth negatively (Romans 3:20, 28; Galatians 2:16; 3:11, 21). Stating it negatively, we would say that God does not justify human beings by works, or by any human effort, including the works of the Law.

In regard to the fundamentals, we too quickly assume that everyone understands what "grace" means. Sadly, most don't know that it means unmerited favor; grace recognizes neither merit nor demerit, and does not depend on either.

> *Grace recognizes neither merit nor demerit, and does not depend on either.*

We also assume that everyone understands what "work" means … but they don't. Therefore, for the sake of clarity (remember Socrates?), let's define *work*. We start with the three attributes or

SCHINDLER'S LIST

Steven Spielberg's 1993 movie, *Schindler's List*, is about the heroic and sacrificial efforts of Oskar Schindler, a German businessman who saved 1,100 Jews from the Holocaust. In a climactic scene, Schindler is standing in the midst of those whom he had kept from the bloody hands of the Nazis. On behalf of the group, his close friend and associate gives him a ring in appreciation for all he's done.

Schindler puts the ring on his finger and says, "If I had made more money. I threw away so much money. You have no idea. If I just...I didn't do enough. This car. Why did I keep the car? Ten people right there. Ten people. Ten more people. This pin...two people. This is gold. It would have given me two more, at least one. One more person. A person...I could have got one more person, and I didn't! I—I—I—I didn't!"

of God He passed over the sins previously committed" (Romans 3:25).

As we read the Old Testament, certainly in reference to the sacrifices, we leave the Old Book with the idea that some big event is coming. We get this feeling not only from the prophets

You'd think we'd get it; the Bible describes the Law as a ministry of death (2 Corinthians 3) and an unkeepable burden (Acts 15). People do not use the Law lawfully when they believe that they're justified or saved by attempting to keep the Ten Commandments. They're placing their faith in the Law and their ability to keep it. The Law, not Christ alone, is the object of their faith.

In Romans 3:20, Paul summarized his argument that any legal code — any code of morality, whether it's the Mosaic Law or a moral code of the gentiles — is unable to justify: "Therefore by the deeds of *the* law there shall no flesh be justified in his sight: for by *the* law is the knowledge of sin." The article "the" (italicized here) is not in the Greek text in either instance. Therefore, Paul is not referring to the specific law of Moses or any other specific code of law. He is including the whole human family in one wide sweep, saying that whatever moral code humankind may be under (that is, whatever law we may be under, whether Jew or gentile), observing such a code will never justify anyone in the sight of God.

Enter the Pharisee

The Pharisees are notorious in world history; their name has become a byword for self-importance, arrogance, and hypocrisy. Eric L. Johnson, associate professor of interdisciplinary studies as Northwestern College, Minnesota, summarizes the Pharisee: "the Pharisees believed they possessed a special standing with God (Matt. 23:6). They thought they were good in God's sight. God had blessed the people of Israel, setting them apart from the pagans, and had given them a set of laws, the following of which guaranteed their special standing" (2018).

The Pharisees seemed to think that this good standing was also a result of their own efforts, what Paul called having "confidence in the flesh" (Philippians 3:3–7). According to Christ's parable of the Pharisee and the tax collector, they may have had some sense that although God was to be *thanked* for their righteousness (Luke 18:11), yet it was ultimately *they* who were to be admired and congratulated for their special standing (Matthew 23:5). God was not so much the source of their goodness as He was the judge and rewarder of *their* good works. They were good because they had worked hard to be good.

The ancient Pharisees entered the boneyard of history long ago, but their legalistic descendants still plague us today. The Pharisees live! The new Pharisees are those who feel superior because of the length of their skirts, their hairstyles, their abstinence from wine and movies, etc., to name only a few. Today's Pharisees raise serious doubts about the genuineness of the faith of other Christians who don't share their voting preferences and behaviors.

When people misunderstand the Law and attempt to keep its commands so as to bring themselves salvation and/or sanctification, they are unwittingly siding with the arrogant Pharisees who strongly opposed the teachings of Christ and His apostles. In doing so, they're using the Law unlawfully, and are among those "wanting to be teachers of the Law, even though they do not understand either what they are saying or the matters about which they make confident assertions" (1 Timothy 1:7).

From the perspective of a biblical theology of missions, the idea that there was no salvation other than that of keeping the Law—i.e., that there was no salvation outside of Israel—is faulty. For example, in Genesis 1–11, God offered salvation long before Israel was established. The author of Hebrews points to Abel, Enoch, Noah, and his family as saved gentiles (Hebrews 11:4, 5, 7). The point is, if gentiles could be saved prior to the giving of the Law when there was no Israel, why could they not be saved after the giving of the Law without coming into Israel? Included among gentile believers after the call of Abraham in Genesis 12 would be Melchizedek, Rahab (while still in Jericho—Hebrews 11:31, living after Mount Sinai), and Ruth, who became a believer while in Moab.

In addition, Paul writes,

> What then? are we [Jews] better than they [the gentiles]? No, in no wise: for we have before proved both Jews and Gentiles, that they are all [Jews and gentiles] under sin ... For all [Jews and gentiles] have sinned, and come short of the glory of God; Being justified freely by his grace through the redemption that is in Christ Jesus. ... Is he the God of the Jews only? Is he not also of the Gentiles? Yes, of the Gentiles also: Seeing it is one God, which shall justify the circumcision [Jews] by faith, and the uncircumcision [gentiles] through faith (Romans 3:9, 23, 24, 29, 30).

Romans 4 holds Abraham up as the pattern for salvation for the human race. How did God justify Abraham? Was it by works of the Law? That was impossible because there was no Mosaic Law in 2,000 BC. So, Paul asks the $64,000 question, "How did God justify Abraham?" How did He declare Abraham righteous? Paul clearly answers the question: "But to the one who does not work, but believes in Him who justifies the ungodly, his faith is credited as righteousness ... Faith was credited to Abraham as righteousness" (Romans 4:5, 9).

Robert L. Deffinbaugh (n.d.), pastor/teacher and elder at Community Bible Chapel, asks,

> Was Abraham saved as a Jew or as a gentile? Was Abraham declared righteous as one who was circumcised or as uncircumcised? Abraham, in Genesis 15:6, was declared righteous on the basis of faith 14 years before he was circumcised (compare Genesis 15:6 with 17:24). Technically, then, Abraham was saved as a gentile, not as a Jew, for he did

not enter Judaism by circumcision, nor did he have the Law to keep. What a blow to the Jew who maintained that one could not be saved without becoming a Jew by circumcision and keeping the Law (Acts 15:1)!

Paul puts David front and center, a man who lived under the Mosaic Law and broke several of the Ten Commandments in one night, then lied and committed murder in the aftermath. How did God justify David? Paul says that David knew how He did it and the Apostle writes: "God credits righteousness apart from works" (Romans 4:6). Comparing the justification of Abraham and the justification of David, we find that the means of their salvation was the same: by faith apart from works.

Getting Specific About Salvation

Since God has never justified anyone, Jew or gentile, by works, including never justifying anyone attempting to keep the Mosaic Law, how were people saved during that dispensation? Or, expanding the question, how were people saved in the time of the Old Testament?

We begin with a first principle: Without faith, it's impossible to please God (Hebrews 11:6). How a person is saved, why a person is saved, and by whom a person is saved has never changed, but the content of faith has necessarily changed because of the nature of progressive revelation.

Salvation has always been by grace through faith in God and His revelation. Salvation has always been by the atonement of Christ, whether in the anticipation of it by faith or the looking back to it by faith. The content of the anticipatory faith and the looking back in faith are what has changed.

> *Salvation has always been by the atonement of Christ.*

When readers open the Old Testament wanting to know the answer, they must be careful that they don't read the New Testament back into the Old. As they read the Old Testament, they realize that they're not coming across the word *gospel*, nor can they find a flat-out definitive statement of the gospel such as one finds in 1 Corinthians 15.

Therefore, what our questioning readers must do is go by the meaning of the word *gospel* and look for any "good news" that God revealed about the coming Deliverer from Genesis to Malachi. They won't read long until they come across Genesis 3:15: "And I will put enmity between you [Satan] and the woman, and between your seed and her seed; He shall bruise you on the head, and you shall bruise Him on the heel."

This was a promise to Adam and Eve which said that the seed of the woman would crush the head of the serpent. That was "gospel"—that is, that was "good news." We see that God is promising the coming of a Person, the Deliverer, because He uses the pronoun "he," "*he* shall bruise you on the head and you shall bruise *him* on the heel." The pronoun is masculine, so God was not promising that Eve would "bruise" the head nor have her heel bruised. Walter Kaiser, Jr. (1978) rightly calls Genesis 3:15 "the mother prophecy" because it gave birth to all the other prophecies.

How do we know that Adam and Eve believed this good news? What Adam did immediately after the promise and the curses doesn't make sense unless they believed the promise of the coming Deliverer: he named his wife "life" or "living" because she was "the mother of all living." What had Adam and Eve just heard God say in the previous verse to his naming of her? They had heard about being dust and returning to dust; they had heard about death, yet Adam names her "life," "living," not "death" and "dying."

To Adam and Eve, God revealed the content of saving faith immediately after the disaster of the Fall. They were to believe the revelation God gave in Genesis 3:15: the Deliverer would come, a Savior who would crush the serpent's head. They didn't know His name; they didn't know where or how or when He would be born; they didn't know that He would die on a cross and be raised from the dead three

> *God's written revelation to the human race was progressive, revealed over time, not all at once.*

days later. This isn't the content of the good news in Genesis 3, but we must remember that God's written revelation to the human race was progressive, revealed over time, not all at once.

> *As God gave more revelation, the content of faith necessarily changed.*

The basis of the atonement has always been the finished work of Christ, either in its anticipation or after its accomplishment. Salvation has always been by grace through faith in God and His revelation, as seen in the progress of revelation. As God gave more revelation, the content of faith necessarily changed. That is, what was believed changed from dispensation to dispensation; as revelation continued, the content of saving faith grew, but the how, why, and in whom remained the same. Those living prior to the cross couldn't be expected to believe what had not yet been revealed.

As revelation progressed, good news was piled upon good news: Genesis 12:1–3, 15:6; Habakkuk 2:4; Job 19:25–27; Psalm 16:9–11; Isaiah 26:19. In Genesis 12:3, we learn that from the "great nation" to come from Abram, "all the families of the earth will be blessed." From Genesis 15:6, we learn that being declared righteous by God comes, not by works, but by faith alone. From Job 19:25–27, the reader would understand that the Redeemer will "take His stand and the earth." From Psalm 16:9–11, David knew that the "Holy One" would not "undergo decay" (cited by Paul and Peter as a prophecy ultimately fulfilled by Jesus Christ). From Habakkuk 2:4, the good news is "the righteous will live by his faith." Isaiah brought more good news in 26:19 when he wrote of a coming resurrection of the dead.

Specifically, What Was Revealed?

What was the content of saving faith during the dispensation of the Law? Unfortunately, many believe that God justified those who generically and generally "believed in God." (This false idea continues today, signifying a faith devoid of meaningful content.) To those who lived during the dispensation of the Law, God had revealed that those who wanted to be justified before Him:

- Must humbly accept their need of justification by accepting God's evaluation of them that they were not good enough (Habakkuk 2:4; Psalm 14:1–3; Ecclesiastes 7:20), to the point of being pronounced sinful and separated from God (Isaiah 59:2).

- Must realize that they lack the necessary righteousness before Him (Psalm 143:2), being so sinful that they are unable to cleanse themselves and justify themselves before Him (Job 9:2, 15:14–16, 25:4–6), their righteousness being pronounced as filthy rags in God's sight (Isaiah 64:6).

- Must recognize that God would have to provide them with salvation (Jonah 2:9) by grace (Isaiah 55:1–3) and cover them with God's own righteousness (Isaiah 61:10).

God commanded all persons, Jews and gentiles, to look only to Him for salvation:

Declare and set forth *your case*; Indeed, let them consult together. Who has announced this from of old? Who has long since declared it? Is it not I, the LORD? And there is no other God besides Me, a righteous God and a Savior; there is none except Me. Turn to Me and be saved, all the ends of the earth; For I am God, and there is no other (Isaiah 45:21–22).

The gentiles are included in this global invitation with the words, "all the ends of the earth." Isaiah instructs the Jew and the gentile to (1) turn to God and (2) be saved. For righteousness, the gentile was to trust not the Mosaic Law, but God.

> *For righteousness, the gentile was to trust not the Mosaic Law, but God.*

To Summarize

Ryrie, in his customary succinct and lucid way, writes, "The requirement for salvation is always the same in any age. Salvation requires faith; the object of that faith is God; the means of salvation is grace; the basis of salvation is the blood of Christ. Only the content of the faith varies" (1995).

Wrap-Up

In John 4:22, Jesus is having conversation with a woman from Samaria who has come to get water from a well. During their dialogue, He tells her that salvation is from the Jews. This would be difficult for her to hear; she's from a highly anti-Semitic group.

Jesus' statement is weighty. The Jews recorded God's program of salvation in the Bible. The knowledge of the content of saving faith (that is, what a person, Jew or gentile, had to believe in order to be saved) came through the Jews. The Savior was a Jew. The first evangelists who declared faith through Christ were Jews.

When considering the Old Testament and salvation, we need to remember that the bulk of the Old Testament deals with the national deliverance of Israel. The emphasis is not on individual salvation, although there are instances of it in Genesis 1–11, and then the examples of Abraham, Melchizedek, Rahab, and Ruth. When the reader comes to the New Testament, things change, as the gospels and the epistles are filled with accounts of individuals whose faith met the right object, Jesus of Nazareth: Andrew, Nathanael, Peter, Nicodemus, the Samaritan woman, a Roman centurion, Zaccheus, Saul, Cornelius, a jailer, and so on.

If Not for Salvation, Then Why?

We must not conclude that the Mosaic Law is a worthless document simply because God didn't give it to teach men how to be saved. Paul alludes to the usefulness of the Law in Romans 7:12, saying that it is "holy, just, and good." In 1 Timothy 1:8, he writes that the Law is good "if one uses it lawfully." Those who lived in the dispensation of the Mosaic Law understood that the Law was holy, just, and good.

God gave the Law to a people already saved. They had applied the blood to their doorposts; the Death Angel had passed over them. When they came to Mount Sinai, they came as immature people, a people who knew they now had a responsibility to

> *God gave the Law to a people already saved.*

Jehovah, but ignorant of what that responsibility was. The Mosaic Law gave to Israel their duties to God as a redeemed people.

J. Dwight Pentecost (1971) states the nine purposes of the Law:

> First, it was given to reveal the holiness of God. Peter writes in 1 Peter 1:15, "But as he which hath called you is holy, so be ye holy in all manner of conversation; because it is written, Be ye holy; for I am holy." The fact that God was a holy God was made very clear to Israel in the Law of Moses. Perhaps the primary function of the Law was to reveal to Israel the

fact of the holiness of God and to make Israel aware of the character of the God who had redeemed them from Egypt.

Continuing on the purposes of the Law, Dr. Pentecost (1971) writes,

> Second, the Mosaic Law was given to reveal or expose the sinfulness of man. It is of this that Paul writes in Galatians 3:19 ... It [the Law] was added because of transgressions, till the seed should come to whom the promise was made; and it was ordained by angels in the hands of a mediator .... But the scripture hath concluded all under sin, that the promise by faith of Jesus Christ might be given to them that believe.

A third purpose of the Law, related to the first two, was to reveal the standard of holiness required of those who had been redeemed in order to enjoy fellowship with God. The Law was given to reveal the standard that God required of those who walk in fellowship with their Redeemer.

A fourth purpose of the Law appears in Galatians 3:24, "Wherefore the law was our schoolmaster ... unto Christ." Pentecost explains that the word schoolmaster (pedagogue) refers to the slave, selected by a child's father, whose responsibility it was to supervise the child's total development: physical, intellectual, and spiritual.

A fifth purpose of the Law is was to act as the unifying principle that made Israel a nation. Exodus 19:5–6 reads, "Now therefore, if ye will obey my voice indeed, and keep my covenant, then ye shall be a peculiar treasure unto me above all people: for all the earth is mine: And ye shall be unto me a kingdom of priests, and an holy nation."

Sixth, one must remember that the Law was given only to Israel, to separate it from everyone else, so that Israel might become a "kingdom of priests." Exodus 31:13 reads: "Speak also unto the children of Israel, saying, You shall surely observe my sabbaths: for it is a sign between Me and you throughout your generations; that you may know that I am the Lord that sanctifies you."

Seventh, the Law was given to a redeemed people to make provision for forgiveness of sins and restoration to fellowship. The same Law that revealed their unworthiness for fellowship also provided for restoration.

Eighth, the Law was given to teach the redeemed people how to worship. In Leviticus 23 the Law set out a cycle of feasts that the nation was expected to observe annually. Through the cycle of feasts, Israel's attention was directed backward to the redemption out of Egypt and forward to the final redemption that would be provided through the Redeemer according to God's promise.

Ninth, the Law provided a test as to whether a person belonged to the kingdom (the theocracy) over which God ruled. The Law thus became a sort of test to reveal whether or not a person was rightly related to God (in God's kingdom): Those who submitted to and obeyed the Law did so because of their faith in God, which produced obedience. Those who disobeyed the Law were presumed to have done so because they were without faith in God, and that lack of faith produced their disobedience.

Finally, it becomes clear from the New Testament that the Law was given to reveal Jesus Christ. The great truths concerning the person and the work of the Lord Jesus Christ are woven throughout the Law, and in fact the Law was given to prepare the nation for the coming Redeemer King. It was because of this that the Lord on the Emmaus road could expound to His companions great truths concerning the Messiah Who had been revealed in the Law.

The Law was given to reveal Jesus Christ.

The Law, Lawfully

So, we've come full circle back to the question with which we began: given that the Law isn't useless, how are we to use the Law lawfully? The Law is holy, just, and good when we use it lawfully, but we don't use it lawfully when we put believers under it.

We use the Law lawfully when we employ the Law to reveal God's holiness. His attribute of holiness doesn't change from dispensation to dispensation. As we use the Law in that holy, just, and good way, we also use it in another good way: to reveal the unholiness of humankind ... because the holiness of God reveals the sinful state of man.

Evangelism begins with a holy God whose character is the measure of all things and thus allows us to identify sin. Beginning with this fundamental principle, the human race learns that there is an absolute right and an absolute wrong. Sin is sin, no matter the time, no matter the location, no matter the culture. This fundamental truth strikes a mortal blow to multiculturalism, relativism, and humans as the measure.

> *Sin is sin, no matter the time, no matter the location, no matter the culture.*

The Law reveals the truth of what Isaiah and Paul said, "All we, like sheep, have gone astray, we have turned, each one to his own way"; that "there is none righteous, no not one; that we have all sinned and are coming short of the glory of God"; that is, we all fall short of God's absolute standard. Paul declares that the Law makes man put his hand over his mouth: "Now we know that whatever the Law says, it speaks to those who are under the Law, so that every mouth may be closed and all the world may become accountable to God" (Romans 3:19). Paul is specific: he refers to "the Law," meaning the Mosaic Law. Jews and even the gentiles, although not under the Law, see their own falling short by means of the Ten Commandments.

Self-Esteem and the Law

This fundamental principle of the unholiness of humans strikes at the heart of man's declaration of himself as God, the ultimate destination of the self-esteem movement. The temptation Satan put to Adam and Eve was self-exaltation with the desired result of becoming "like God" (Genesis 3:5). We find this drive to be God in cults such as the Church of Jesus Christ of Latter Day Saints, the Mormons. One of the best-known couplets of Mormonism is, "As man is, God once was; as God is, man may be." This is a lie that Satan has perpetuated since Eden; he knows that fallen man loves to hear it as he lives east of Eden.

The Jehovah's Witnesses state: "We are divine beings—hence all such are Gods ... it is claiming that we are divine beings— hence all such are Gods." (*Watchtower*, 1881).

These cults are self-esteem on steroids. Instead of building self-esteem, the Bible commands something different: "For if anyone thinks he is something when he is nothing, he deceives himself" (Galatians 6:3). "For through the grace given to me I say to every man among you not to think more highly of himself than he ought to think; but to think so as to have sound judgment, as God has allotted to each a measure of faith" (Romans 12:3). We are also instructed to "[d]o nothing from selfishness or empty conceit, but with humility of mind let each of you regard one another as more important than himself; do not merely look out for your own personal interests, but also for the interests of others" (Philippians 2:3, 4).

Typology

We use the Law lawfully by using the types in the sacrificial system to point to Christ. One example is the Passover lamb as a type of Christ as the Lamb of God, as Paul says, "Christ our Passover has been sacrificed for us" (1 Corinthians 5:7). We may not remember that the backstory of the Passover, as recorded in Exodus 12, is that the tenth plague to come on the land was to come on both the Egyptians *and* the Jews unless the blood of a lamb was on their doors.

God does not take delight in any human's death. In regard to the coming plague, God extended His grace: He warned both the Egyptians and the Jews beforehand that the judgment was coming, even specifying the day and the time of day as being about midnight of April 14, 1400 BC (ca.):

> Moses said, Thus says the Lord, "About midnight I am going out into the midst of Egypt, and all the firstborn in the land of Egypt shall die, from the firstborn of the Pharaoh who sits on his throne, even to the firstborn of the slave girl who is behind the millstones; all the firstborn of the cattle as well. Moreover, there shall be a great cry in all the land of Egypt, such as there has not been before and such as shall never be again" (Exodus 11:4–6).

Then, in grace, God instructed the Israelites on the way—the one way, the only way—to escape what was coming: if they sacrificed a lamb and painted its blood on the two side posts and the upper post of their door, He promised, "The blood shall be a sign for you on the houses where you live; and when I see the blood I will pass over you, and no plague will befall you to destroy you when I strike the land of Egypt" (Exodus 12:13).

Just as Israel and Egypt were under a death sentence because of our being in Adam at the Fall (Romans 5), so all of us stand under God's death sentence upon us because we have a sin nature (Ephesians 2:1 3) and we have all committed acts of personal sin. Judgment is coming, but it won't be in this life (Hebrews 9:27; Revelation 20:13 15). By the very force of those two Scriptures, the human race has been forewarned, just as God alerted the Jews and the Egyptians.

God's grace extends to us, every man, woman, and child, just as it did in Egypt — God provided the way — the only way, the one way — to avoid the coming judgment: Jesus Christ, the Son of God. The way to avoid the judgment in Egypt was to apply the blood of the lamb to one's door posts. When the Jews smeared the blood on the door posts, it was an outward symbol of their inner faith in and obedience to what God had said about the efficacy of the blood of the lamb.

It remains to us today to trust what God has said about His Lamb, the Lamb to end all lambs: "The next day he [John the Baptist] saw Jesus coming to him and said, 'Behold, the Lamb of God who takes away the sin of the world'!" (John 1:29).

In Exodus 12:3, we learn that *each one* who wanted to be saved needed to be within a household with a sacrificial lamb. No one died that night because he needed a lamb. God didn't mock the Jews by requiring something they couldn't do. If their firstborn died that night, it would be because there was no lamb's blood on his doorposts, not because he had no lamb.

In just the same way, God has provided the Lamb who died for the sins of every person who has ever lived or will ever live on this planet: "... He Himself is the propitiation [satisfaction] for our sins; and not for ours only, but also for *those of* the whole world (1 John 2:2). 1 Timothy 2:5–6 records: "For there is one God and one mediator between God and men, the man Christ Jesus, who gave himself as a ransom for *all* men — the testimony given in its proper time." The author of Hebrews declares: "But we see Jesus, who was made a little lower than the angels, now crowned with glory and honor because he suffered death, so that by the grace of God he might taste death *for everyone*" (2:9).

Scrutiny to the Max

When an Israelite selected a lamb for that coming day, he had to be careful which one he chose, because it had to be perfect to be acceptable before God. The animal couldn't be blind, or have a crooked nose, or a broken hoof, or any broken bones; it could not have any boils, scabs, scars, or scurvy on its skin — its wool must be fleecy white (Leviticus 22:22–24).

But those criteria didn't end the matter. According to Exodus 12:3, the lamb was selected on the tenth day: "Speak to all the congregation of Israel saying, 'On the tenth of this month they are each one to take a lamb for themselves, according to their fathers' households, a lamb for each household.'" Then, the owner was to observe the lamb for four days to make certain it had no disqualifying defect: "You shall keep it until the fourteenth day of the same month" (Exodus 12:6).

God's Lamb, Jesus Christ, spent the three years of His public ministry under the intense glare of Pharisaic, public, priestly, and Sadducean examination. Prior to the beginning of His public ministry, God's verdict on His Son was, "I am well pleased" (Matthew 3:17). During His public ministry, Jesus publicly demanded, "Which one of you convicts Me of sin?" (John 8:46) Their silence answered His question: No one. At His Transfiguration, again, the Father's pronouncement on the life of His Son was, "I am well pleased" (Matthew 17:5). So, at various points in His earthly ministry, Jesus was pronounced perfect.

Judas, who had observed Him up close and personal for three years, said of Him, "I have sinned by betraying [His] innocent blood." If someone were to observe you and me for three years, would he be able to declare us innocent? Of course not. But let's refine the question to ask, "Would one of our *enemies*, who would be on the lookout for *any* sin at all, be able to declare us innocent after having spent three years with us?" Of course not; he would have a huge laundry list of our offenses against both God and man. But Judas, at the very end, pronounces Jesus, "Innocent!"

The centurion who witnessed the crucifixion began to praise God and said, "Certainly this man was innocent" (Luke 23:47). The highest-ranking gentile official in Israel concurred, rendering his judicial verdict by declaring to the chief priests and to the crowds, "I find no guilt in this man" (Luke 23:4).

Peter, who was in a close relationship with Jesus, travelling with Him, eating with Him, observing Him in situations both calm and tense, wrote about Him that He "committed no sin, nor was any deceit found in His mouth." The word *committed* is in the aorist tense, meaning, "He committed not one single instance of sin." When Peter wrote, "Nor was any deceit *found* in His mouth," he used a Greek word meaning "to find after close examination."

Neither friends nor a host of foes could rightly accuse Him of any sin. When His enemies did accuse Him of sin, the charges were lies by "witnesses" who couldn't agree with one another in court. The Gospels record the corruption of the court by asserting that the Jewish authorities "kept trying to obtain false testimony against Jesus" (Matthew 26:59).

Is the impeccability of God's Lamb important? You bet it is! Only a perfect Person, the God-Man substituting for us, could pay the penalty for our sins. Had Jesus been a sinner, He would have needed someone to pay for His sins. The impeccability of Jesus Christ is also important because God says that when a person trusts Christ alone for eternal life, God clothes that person with the righteousness of the sinless Christ, the righteousness we must have in order to live with God forever.

No Broken Bones About It

We do need to note that little detail in Exodus 12:46: [The Passover lamb] "is to be eaten in a single house; you are not to bring forth any of the flesh outside of the house, nor are you to break any bone of it." Fourteen hundred years later, at the crucifixion, although the soldiers broke the legs of the two crucified thieves to hasten their demise, they didn't break Jesus' legs because He was already dead.

Faith in What God Has Said

When the Israelite painted his door posts, this was an outward sign of the inward reality of his faith in the blood of a lamb to save him. It was an outward sign that his trust was in what God had declared about the blood of the lamb and nothing else. In this same way, to have eternal life, our trust must be in what God has declared concerning the precious blood of His Son Jesus Christ: that His death completely finished paying for our sins.

Dr. Bruce Waltke (2012a, b) describes our trust in Christ:

> Methodist Bishop Munsey tells an allegory that vividly describes faith. He pictures a man who was walking along, not particularly minding where he was going. As he was walking along in this preoccupied state of mind, suddenly he fell off the edge of a cliff and found himself falling to a certain death. Fortunately, however, as he hurtled down he reached out and grabbed hold of a limb that was jutting out of the cliff-like rock. As he grasped this limb holding him, suspended as it were, between life and death, an angel suddenly appeared to him. In his desperation the man cried out to the angel asking him to save him. The angel responded by asking, "Do you believe I can save you?" Having observed the obvious strength of the angel, the man cried back, "Yes, I believe you can save me." Then the angel asked, "Do you

believe I will save you?" Seeing the grace and kindness that radiated in the angel's face, the man cried out, "Yes, I believe you will save me." The angel then replied, "Let go." That's a perfect illustration of what faith in Christ involves. It means to let go of everything else you may be trusting and trust only him to save you. It means to let go of your faith in your own good works; it means to let go of the religion and traditions in which you may have been reared. Let go of everything and trust only Jesus Christ.

Precision of the Day and Time, 1,400 Years Later

Dr. Waltke (2012a, b) writes of the time of the sacrifice of the Passover lamb:

At the end of Exodus 12:6 it is recorded, "Then the whole assembly of the congregation of Israel is to kill it at twilight." ... Actually, the Hebrew says, "between the evenings." According to the best Jewish authorities (Josephus, the Talmud, the Midrash, etc.), the phrase "between the evenings" refers to that period of time between 3 o'clock and 6 o'clock in the evening.

Now it was exactly at this time of the day that our Lord was crucified upon the cross. Not only was he slain at the same time of the day that the Passover lamb was slain, but he was probably put to death upon the cross on the very day that the Passover lamb was slain. From John 18:28 we are led to believe that the Jews would eat the Passover on the very day that Jesus Christ was crucified. "Then they led Jesus from Caiaphas into the Praetorium so that they would not be defiled, but might eat the Passover." That he died between 3:00 and 6:00 in the evening is clear from Matthew 27:46: "About the ninth hour [i.e., our 3:00 p.m.] Jesus cried out with a loud voice, saying, ... 'My God, my God, why have you forsaken me?'" Finally, in Matthew 27:50, which is sometime later, we read: "And Jesus cried out again with a loud voice, and yielded up his spirit." From these verses we conclude then that Jesus Christ died at exactly the same time the Passover lamb was slain in perfect fulfillment of the type.

So you see, Christ was similar to the Passover lamb because he, too, was slain by the whole congregation of Israel, was without blemish, and died at precisely the same time as the Passover lamb.

Peter succinctly makes the Passover an analogy to Christ, writing, "knowing that you were not redeemed with perishable things like silver or gold from your futile way of life inherited from your forefathers, but with precious blood, as of a lamb unblemished and spotless, *the blood* of Christ" (1 Peter 1:18–19). The question for you is this: Have you trusted in the sacrifice of God's Lamb and that sacrifice alone, letting go of your works, the Law, your religion, and the religious works and traditions therein? If not, why not?

Only the sovereign God revealed in the Bible could have worked out the minute details of the Passover lamb to be fulfilled by His Son. No human being, especially not the disciples, could have "rigged" these details to be not merely fulfilled, but precisely, down to the smallest detail, fulfilled 1,400 years later.

The God of the Bible is the God of the universe and the God of the details!

6

Lay Down the Law

The purpose of this chapter is to free you from the Mosaic Law, a freedom that will bring you the liberty God wants you to enjoy in the Christian life. This liberty will mean freedom from pressurized and enforced tithing, freedom from restricted activities on Sunday, freedom from legalistic dress codes, and freedom from the guilt put upon you by an army of pastors, evangelists, Sunday school teachers, and the hypocritical Christian in the next pew.

First Things First

When we speak of laying down the Law, we're referring to the Mosaic Law in its entirety: the whole thing, even the Ten Commandments. At first blush, this sounds heretical because it flies in the face of what you've heard all your ecclesiastical life, but bear with me; let's reason through this together.

The first truth to recognize is that the Mosaic Law was a complete, unified package revealed to Israel by God. The Jew was under the whole thing, all 613 commands, not just the Ten Commandments. An Israelite had no right to say, "I'll be under this law, but not that law," any more than we can say, "I'll observe the 65 mile-per-hour speed limit on the interstate, but I refuse to be under the 20 mile-per-hour speed limit in the school zones." We can't choose the laws we want to keep. If we do, we'll pay the fines and penalties that go with the laws we break.

To help us see that the Law is an all-or-nothing complete package, all we have to do is ask one question: Is there any scriptural basis for separating the Ten Commandments from the other 603 and declaring the Big Ten to be "forever" laws and not the hundreds of others?

How can we say that the Law is a complete and unified package? We can say that by looking at the grammar of the Hebrew Old Testament and the Greek grammar of the New. In the Old Testament, as we've seen, the Law consists of 613 laws, yet what word does the Old Testament use for those 613 statutes? It uses the singular, "the Law" (Torah) not the plural, "the laws." When we turn to the New Testament, we see the same grammar; the word of choice when the New Testament authors refer to the Mosaic Law is *nomos*, "law." Singular.

Can We Do to the Law What Caesar Did to Gaul?

Julius Caesar began his commentary on the Gallic Wars by writing, "All Gaul is divided into three parts." You may be thinking, "But I've heard that the Law can be divided into three parts: the ceremonial, moral, and the legal." You'd be correct, but that's done for our convenience. The Bible never makes such a division.

James 2:10 is a plain statement about the unity of the Mosaic Law: "For whoever keeps the whole law and yet stumbles in *one point*, he has become guilty of all." James is saying that if you lined up all the 613 laws in the Mosaic Law and you (hypothetically of course) kept 612 of them, but couldn't keep the 613th, you'd be guilty of breaking the entire Mosaic Law.

Let's say an Israelite broke the law of Deuteronomy 22:8: "When you build a new house, you shall make a parapet [a low, protective wall] for your roof, so that you will not bring bloodguilt on your house if anyone falls from it." Because the Law is a unit, the Israelite who didn't install a parapet would be guilty of breaking the Ten Commandments, even though none of the Ten Commandments says anything about home construction.

The point of all this is that the Mosaic Law cannot be divided into parts of which we can say, "This part stays, while that part goes." It either all stays or it all goes, because it is a package

> **The Mosaic Law cannot be divided into parts.**

deal, a single unit. This principle also applies to the various commandments: they all stay or they all go.

Paul argued the same point in Galatians. There were false teachers who were corrupting the gospel of grace by importing the Mosaic Law into it. These teachers were clever; they had led many of the Galatian believers away from grace and into the Mosaic Law with their teaching. Paul wrote to the Galatians, advising, "And I testify again to every man who receives circumcision, that he is under obligation to keep the whole Law" (Galatians 5:3).

Paul is saying that if a Christian decides to put himself under one single solitary law of the Mosaic Law (circumcision, in this case) in order to be accepted by God by keeping that one Mosaic law, then he must put himself under the entire Mosaic Law, which would include constructing the roof of his house with a parapet, restricting his activities on Saturday (the Sabbath), excluding ham from his diet, and observing all the other laws. Paul builds an airtight case for the unity of the Mosaic Law in that one sentence.

Paul is demonstrating to the Galatian Christians that they cannot be consistent in putting themselves under the Law to ensure a right standing before God. That's what legalism does; it breeds judgmental, self-righteous, hypocritical, and inconsistent Christians.

We can see the inconsistency that Mosaic Law-keeping brings by turning to Leviticus 20:13: "If there is a man who lies with a male as those who lie with a woman, both of them have committed a detestable act; they shall surely be put to death. Their bloodguiltiness is upon them." If we are under the Mosaic Law, then execution for homosexuality is a command to be obeyed by our culture. However, in the very same chapter, we find laws against eating unclean animals and the prescription of the death penalty for any youth rebelling against his father or mother, yet these aren't seen as normative for our culture.

Furthermore, in Leviticus 19:18, we read, "Love your neighbor as yourself," while in the next verse we read that one isn't to wear cloth woven from two different kinds of material. Inconsistently, 19:18 is held as applicable to us today, whereas 19:19 is not.

In Deuteronomy 22:5, we read, "A woman shall not wear men's clothing," while in the same list we read that one is not to plant two kinds of seeds in the same vineyard (vs. 9) and that one is to wear tassels on the four corners of one's cloak (vs. 12). Here we have two dress code laws: many consider the one in verse 5 applicable/mandatory whereas the one seven verses later is arbitrarily deemed inapplicable.

Legalism turns Christians into ugly, self-righteous, judgmental believers, people who are unattractive because they have come to believe that God approves of them because they keep their own nonscriptural traditions and rules, while judging and looking down upon those who don't, even to the point of pronouncing them as either having lost their salvation or never having had it.

An independent, fundamental American Baptist church published the following list of qualifications for its church workers. If a person violated any item on the list, he or she was to repent and correct the slip; failing that, either resign their position or be stripped of it. The list included:

- Failure to tithe; failing to attend church or being late for church; watching movies that are not G-rated; listening to country-western, rock, rap, or contemporary Christian music; using tobacco, alcohol, or nonmedicinal drugs.

- For men, wearing shorts; having hair that fell below the collar or was not cut above the ears; wearing an earring or a necklace; going without a shirt; wearing "unisex" fashions; or failing to trim a mustache or sideburns.

- For women, wearing shorts or pants; having short hair; wearing a skirt that does not completely cover the knees; wearing a skirt with a split hem; wearing a blouse with a low neckline or any sort of see-through clothing; or wearing heavy makeup.

We see the power of legalists in the following example, as told by Randal Rauser (2014):

A couple years ago a colleague of mine shared an example of Christian legalism from his youth. It was the 1960s, a small town in the American heartland. Given that there wasn't too much to do you might have thought the family would have been anxious to see "The Sound of Music" when it came to town. But while the family did indeed want to see the movie, they didn't want the social stigma of being seen at the worldly movie theater, and so *they drove forty-five minutes to the next town* so they could attend that theater anonymously.

A man, 88 years of age, recalled the legalism of his family, confessing, "I remember when *Bambi* came to town we had to drive to Calgary to see it. We had a theater in our hometown, but we couldn't deal with the scandal of being seen going there."

In the early 1980s, the students of a Bible college had to be circumspect when they went to a movie theater, as some of the college staff would always be driving back and forth in the area to catch or report on anyone from the student body going into the theater.

These examples of the power of legalists demonstrate how people will bow to their rules. In many church situations, the legalists always win.

Now, Lay Down the Law

Earlier, we saw how God laid down the Mosaic Law at Mount Sinai, but in this chapter we're using *"laying down* the Law" in a different sense. We're saying let it go: lay it down because the Law was abolished as a rule of life for the Christian by the Grace Dispensation.

> **Law was abolished as a rule of life for the Christian by the Grace Dispensation.**

We have a large body of scriptural evidence upon which to make such a claim.

"For Christ is the **end** of the law for righteousness to everyone who believes." The word "end" is *telos*, a word which every Greek lexicon says means "end," as in "termination"; both Thayer's lexicon (1978) and Arndt and Gingrich (1957) give this as the primary meaning. Arndt and Gingrich give the primary meaning of the verb form of *telos* as "bring to an end, finish, complete." Romans 10:4 says, "For sin shall not be master over you, for you are not under law but under grace." In Romans 6:14, Paul shows that there is an antithetical relationship between law and grace, a difference that is irreconcilable. The one cannot be compatible with the other, a teaching also found in John's prologue (John 1:17).

> Or do you not know, brethren (for I am speaking to those who know the law), that the law has jurisdiction over a person as long as he lives? [2] For the married woman is bound by law to her husband while he is living; but if her husband dies, she is released from the law concerning the husband. [3] So then, if while her husband is living she is joined to another man, she shall be called an adulteress; but if her husband dies, she is free from the law, so that she is not an adulteress though she is joined to another man.

> Therefore, my brethren, you also were made to die to the Law through the body of Christ, so that you might be joined to another, to Him who was raised from the dead, in order that we might bear fruit for God. [5] For while we were in the flesh, the sinful passions, which were *aroused* by the Law, were at work in the members of our body to bear fruit for death. [6] But now *we have been released from the Law*, having died to that by which we were bound, so that we serve in newness of the Spirit and not in oldness of the letter. (Romans 7:1–6)

Paul clearly says that the Law has no authority over a person. In his marriage analogy, Paul points out that once the death of the husband takes place, his wife is free to remarry; their marriage relationship has no more claims upon her. She's free. Any vows she took, any promises she made, any loyalty she owed, and any responsibilities she had are now canceled and no longer operative. Any claims he had on her are abrogated upon his death.

In his theological analogy, Paul says that such a death—the death of Christ— has taken place, and therefore we are no longer bound by the Law; the death of Christ discharges us from any and all obligations to it. Believers are now married to Christ; it's impossible for them to be married to both Christ and the Law.

> [9] On the next day, as they were on their way and approaching the city, Peter went up on the housetop about the sixth hour to pray. [10] But he became hungry and was desiring to eat; but while they were making preparations, he fell into a trance; [11] and he saw the sky opened up, and an object like a great sheet coming down, lowered by four corners to the ground, [12] and there were in it all *kinds of* four-footed animals and crawling creatures of the earth and birds of the air. [13] A voice came to him, "Get up, Peter, kill and eat!" [14] But Peter said, "By no means, Lord, for I have never eaten anything unholy and unclean." [15] Again a voice *came* to him a second time, "What God has cleansed, no *longer* consider unholy." [16] This happened three times, and immediately the object was taken up into the sky. (Acts 10:9–16)

That the Mosaic Law which had governed Israel for 1,500 years was gone was a difficult lesson for the early church to learn. Peter, refusing to do what God told him to do three times, demonstrates the continuing power that the diet prescribed in the Law (Leviticus 11) had on him. The Law had declared certain foods to be unclean and off the menu of devout Jews. Yet, as of the death of Christ, the Law was abolished and Peter had no obligation to obey Leviticus 11. Peter needed to learn that in the Grace Dispensation no food was off the menu; all foods were now clean.

That the Mosaic Law which had governed Israel for 1,500 years was gone was a difficult lesson for the early church to learn.

Peter also learned an important lesson as he stated in Acts 10:28–29: "And he said to them, 'You yourselves know how unlawful it is for a man who is a Jew to associate with a foreigner or to visit him; and yet God has shown me that I should not call any man unholy or unclean. That is why I came without even raising any objection when I was sent for.'"

"Why the Law then? It was added because of transgressions, having been ordained through angels by the agency of a mediator, until the seed would come to whom the promise had been made" (Galatians 3:19).

In his discussion of the Law, Paul notes that it was a temporary arrangement for Israel from its inception; there was an "until" in Israel's acceptance of the Law and that "until" was "until the seed would come." The Law was an addition alongside the Abrahamic Covenant and its purpose was

The seed was Christ: now that He has suffered and died, the Law has been terminated.

to make sin crystal clear so that Israel would know that they had fallen short of God's requirements for righteousness. The seed was Christ: now that He has suffered and died, the Law has been terminated.

"Therefore the Law has become our tutor *to lead us* to Christ, so that we may be justified by faith. But now that faith has come, we are no longer under a tutor" (Galatians 3:24–25). Unfortunately, "tutor" doesn't give the Greek word *paidagogos* its due, and that's because we don't have anyone quite like the "tutor" in our society today. But the Greeks did and Paul took the word *paidagogos* (παιδαγωγος) and used it in a way like no one else.

In Michael J. Smith's word study (2006), he writes that the *paidagogos* wasn't a tutor; he gave no formal education. If and when he taught, he did so indirectly and only by supervision. He was a special slave in the ancient household, usually there because he was a prisoner of war. Plato thought highly of those who occupied the position. The paidagogos had to be a very responsible person because it was to him that the parents gave the complete oversight of their son at the age of seven. Nevertheless, that oversight was temporary; when the boy reached late adolescence, the family no longer required the services of the paidagogos. Those services were to escort the boy to and from school, to carry his books and whatever else he needed, to take him to sports practice, to oversee his meals, to make him do his homework, to protect him, to see to the child's moral development, to punish him when needed, to correct his grammar, to ensure proper diction, and to supervise his social life. The paidagogos monitored the boy's life 24/7. The paidagogos was a drone, keeping the youth under his untiring watchful eye.

Paul uses the paidagogos's relationship to the child as a metaphor for the Law's relationship to Israel. No one had ever done that before. In Jewish literature, Smith (2006) found that the authors referred to Moses, Aaron, Miriam, David, and Jeremiah as holding such a position over Israel, but never do they refer to the Law in that relationship over Israel.

According to Smith, we see the reason Paul applies *paidagogos* to the Law in the last part of verse 24: the Law was to lead Israel *until* Christ. The Greek word "to" ["until"] Christ, has a temporal sense and this fits the context of Galatians 3:19–4:7. With the death of Christ, the "until" had come; there was then a change in dispensations.

The paidagogos was for children, for the immature. For an adult to put himself back under his paidagogos would be to revert to childhood. Who would do that?

> Therefore remember that formerly you, the Gentiles in the flesh, who are called "Uncircumcision" by the so-called "Circumcision," *which is* performed in the flesh by human hands—*remember* that you were at that time separate from

Christ, excluded from the commonwealth of Israel, and strangers to the covenants of promise, having no hope and without God in the world. But now in Christ Jesus you who formerly were far off have been brought near by the blood of Christ. For He Himself is our peace, who made both *groups into* one and broke down the barrier of the dividing wall, *by abolishing in His flesh the enmity, which is the Law of commandments contained in ordinances*, so that in Himself He might make the two into one new man, thus establishing peace, and might reconcile them both in one body to God through the cross, by it having put to death the enmity. (Ephesians 2:11–16)

The Law had created a barrier between Jew and gentile. This separation created hostility between the two groups. Paul says that the barrier, the Law, was "rendered inoperative" at the cross; no longer did it govern the life of the Jew. It was the entire Law, the "Law of commandments" which Christ's death rendered inoperative, not simply a part of the Law.

But if the ministry of death, in letters engraved on stones, came with glory, so that the sons of Israel could not look intently at the face of Moses because of the glory of his face, fading *as* it was, ⁸ how will the ministry of the Spirit fail to be even more with glory? For if the ministry of condemnation has glory, much more does the ministry of righteousness abound in glory. For indeed what had glory, in this case has no glory because of the glory that surpasses *it*. For if that which fades away *was* with glory, much more that which remains *is* in glory. (2 Corinthians 3:7–11)

Once again, Paul is crystal clear: even the Ten Commandments, which many hold onto as permanent, are abolished, for they were the "letters engraved on stones." They have been replaced by that which does not condemn, but brings life and justification.

How does the Law bring condemnation and death? It condemns those who approach it by trying to keep it in order to produce a good standing before God. The condemnation is in the inability of the one coming to the Law to earn righteousness by works.

> Now if perfection was through the Levitical priesthood (for on the basis of it the people received the Law), what further need *was there* for another priest to arise according to the order of Melchizedek, and not be designated according to the order of Aaron? 12 For when the priesthood is changed, of necessity there takes place a change of law also. (Hebrews 7:11–12)

The author points out that the Levitical priesthood was the basis of the Mosaic Law. That priesthood is gone. As stated in a previous chapter, if the basis of the Law is gone, would not the Law itself be gone? When the priesthood changed, there was a change of law also. Christ is our high priest today. If the Mosaic Law is still in effect, Christ is not our high priest. To say it another way, if Christ is our high priest, then the Law cannot be binding on us.

> Some men came down from Judea and *began* teaching the brethren, "Unless you are circumcised according to the custom of Moses, you cannot be saved." 2 And when Paul and Barnabas had great dissension and debate with them, *the brethren* determined that Paul and Barnabas and some others of them should go up to Jerusalem to the apostles and elders concerning this issue. 3 Therefore, being sent on their way by the church, they were passing through both Phoenicia and Samaria, describing in detail the conversion of the Gentiles, and were bringing great joy to all the brethren. 4 When they arrived at Jerusalem, they were received by the church and the apostles and the elders, and they reported all that God had done with them. 5 But some of the sect of the Pharisees who had believed stood up, saying, "It is necessary to circumcise

them and to direct them to observe the Law of Moses." (Acts 15:1–5)

Just as it does today, the attempt to put believers under the bondage of the Law, either for salvation or sanctification, brings about "great dissension and debate." The apostles and the elders called a meeting to argue against the false teachers. Peter, Barnabas, Paul, and James carry the day and lead the church to conclude that the Law was a yoke neither their ancestors nor they could bear; that to put believers under the Law would trouble them; that to lay the Law on them would be a burden; that Jews and gentiles were saved "by the grace of the Lord Jesus," and not by trying to keep the Mosaic Law.

> *Jews and gentiles were saved "by the grace of the Lord Jesus," and not by trying to keep the Mosaic Law.*

The Time Factor

The Mosaic Law was only for Israel in that time period, living in that place. For example, the Law cannot be applied in any nation today in regard to capital punishment. Today, there are two different ways to convict someone of premeditated murder. One of those ways is by circumstantial evidence, involving modern science and forensics. One killer moved a teapot at his victim's home, leaving his fingerprints to prove he was at the scene of the crime. Another murderer's clothing held residual microscopic evidence that was transferred from the victim onto his shirt, which put him at the scene of the crime. DNA evidence found under the victim's fingernails has merited a death sentence for many a murderer, even when (as is usually the case) there were no eyewitnesses to the crimes.

In sharp contrast, under the Mosaic Law, circumstantial evidence carried no weight. A conviction and the death penalty could be meted out if, and only if, there were at least two eyewitnesses to the crime. One eyewitness to a murder would not suffice to cause execution of the accused (Numbers 35:30; Deuteronomy 17:6, 19:15). This provision of the Law would have made capital punishment a rarity in Israel.

If the Law were to be implemented in modern society, and the death penalty were to be enforced in America, the witnesses whose testimony had enabled the guilty verdict would have to participate in the execution by throwing the

> **The Mosaic Law was for Israel then, but not America now or ever.**

first stones; after that, the community as a whole would have to participate as well (Deuteronomy 17:7).

The Mosaic Law was for Israel then, but not America now or ever.

But There's This Problem

When we turn to Acts 21, many see an inconsistent apostle: Paul, the champion of grace, went to the temple, purified himself for temple worship, and showed his support of the Jewish custom by paying for the offerings of the four Jewish men who accompanied him.

As always, there's a context, a backstory, which helps us understand what's happening. There were certain Jewish believers who had heard that Paul was instructing Jewish converts not to practice circumcision or to observe the Jewish customs. The report was false; what Paul was teaching—and rightly so—was that observing those customs was unnecessary for justification and for sanctification.

Paul never objected to circumcision, which was based on the Abrahamic Covenant, because circumcision was the sign of that covenant and therefore the Jews should observe that sign;

however, they were to do so on the basis of the Abrahamic Covenant, not the Mosaic Law. We see in Acts 16:3 that Paul had Timothy circumcised, and could rightly do so as a sign of God's covenant with Abraham and his descendants. This would not in any way violate Paul's preaching the doctrine of faith alone in Christ alone for a right standing before God.

But what about Paul's taking a Jewish vow and observing the purification rites before worshipping in the Temple? What about Paul's being involved in paying for the offerings of the four Jewish men, as was suggested to him? What about the vow Paul took in Acts 18:18: "Paul, having remained many days longer, took leave of the brethren and put out to sea for Syria, and with him were Priscilla and Aquila. In Cenchrea he had his hair cut, for he was keeping a vow."

It appears that C. I. Scofield, in the *Scofield Reference Bible* (1909), sees Paul as inconsistent when he took the vow: a vow based on Numbers 6:2, 5, 9, and 18, which would be part of the Mosaic Law. Scofield put Acts 18:18 under the subheading of "The author of Rom. 6:14; II Cor. 3:7–14; and Galatians 3:23–28 takes a Jewish vow."

But was the apostle of grace being inconsistent? Not at all. To understand what Paul is doing here, remember that although the believer is free from the Law, he's also free to keep parts of it. Let's look at it this way. Say you read over the dietary laws of Israel and, for the sake of health—*not* salvation—you decide to observe those laws: you abstain from ham, from shrimp, and from any or all of the restricted foods and eat only what's on the Jewish menu. You are free to do that.

Let's further say that you want to plan your giving to the Lord's work and you realize you're free to decide the amount (let's say a percentage of your income) that you want to give. Let's say you settle on 10%, a tithe. You're free to do that, or you can decide on 9% or 11%, ... whatever.

You can decide to keep parts of the Law, *as long as you don't think that you're meriting a right standing before God* thereby. If you think you're gaining Brownie points in the service of the Lord by keeping some of the Law, you're using the Law unlawfully, as we've seen. If you think that you're gaining a right standing before God, based on your keeping a part of it, then Paul would say, "Wait. Then you've got to keep the whole thing." And that, as we have seen, is neither effective nor even possible.

> **You can decide to keep parts of the Law, as long as you don't think that you're meriting a right standing before God thereby.**

If you decide to give 10% of your income, do not expect or demand that others to do the same. Do not judge others on the basis of your choices. It's at this point many believers become ugly believers. We must respect the freedom of other believers in such matters — a fellow Christian has the freedom not to keep the Law. We aren't to judge or condemn one another in this. It's to be "Live and let live."

In summary, Paul decided to keep parts of the Law, but not in order to gain a right standing before God, nor did he condemn others for not doing as he did. We must also recognize that Paul lived to bring the grace message, faith alone in Christ alone. To do that, he conducted himself by this principle: "To the Jews I became as a Jew, so that I might win Jews; to those who are under the Law, as under the Law though not being myself under the Law, so that I might win those who are under the Law" (1 Corinthians 9:20).

The New Law

The first reaction that many have upon hearing that the believer of the Grace Dispensation is not under the rule of the Mosaic

When I attended the Day of Atonement service at a Jewish temple, a kind usher handed me a skullcap to wear inside the building. I wore it because of 1 Corinthians 9:20. I was observing a Jewish custom so as not to needlessly offend my hosts. I didn't wear the cap thinking that it would bring me any merit before God whatsoever.

Law is to declare in amazement, "Then that means it's all right to lie or even murder. Surely not!" But what the questioner doesn't understand is that, although believers in the Grace Dispensation aren't under the Mosaic Law, they're not lawless.

According to Galatians 6:2, we are under a new law, the Law of Christ, also called "the law of the Spirit of Life" (Romans 8:2). This Law is distinct from the Mosaic Law and is only for the believer in our present dispensation; it was never in effect until the Grace Age began in Acts 2.

Although believers in the Grace Dispensation aren't under the Mosaic Law, they're not lawless.

Basically, the Law of Christ comprises all the commands of the epistles. Therefore, we are far, far from lawless.

Nine of the Ten Commandments come into the Grace Age in a modified fashion. The following study of the Ten Commandments and their restatement in the New Testament is based on the research of Dr. Roy L. Aldrich (1961).

The First Three Commandments

"You shall have no other gods before Me.

For this new age, we find that nine of the Ten Commandments are included in the Law of Christ, restated according to the principles of grace in the epistles. Under the Law of Christ, Paul restates the first of the Ten Commandments in 1 Timothy 2:5: "For there is one God, and one mediator between God and man, the man Christ Jesus" and we find in James 2:19: "You believe that God is one. You do well; the demons also believe, and shudder." But note well, no author of the New Testament says that the penalty for the violation of this first commandment is the death penalty. Therefore, we could say that the principle of the first of the Ten Commandments is restated in the Law of Christ, but in line with grace.

The second command in the Mosaic Law's Ten Commandments is that the Israelite was not to make any graven image of Yahweh; Deuteronomy 27:15 prescribes death for the offender. This command is incorporated into the Law of Christ without the capital punishment penalty for violation. We see its inclusion in Acts 15:29; 1 Corinthians 8:1–10, 12:2; 2 Corinthians 6:16; and 1 John 5:21. Again we see that although the second commandment has been abolished, the moral principle underlying it has been retained in the Law of Christ.

The third commandment stipulated, "You shall not take the name of the LORD your God in vain, for the LORD will not leave him unpunished who takes His name in vain." The Mosaic Law's penalty for breaking this law was death: "the one who blasphemes the name of the LORD shall surely be put to death;

all the congregation shall certainly stone him. The alien as well as the native, when he blasphemes the Name, shall be put to death" (Leviticus 24:15–16). No such penalty is ever stated in Acts or the epistles.

Dr. Aldrich notes:

> In the New Testament the principle of the third commandment is expanded to include simplicity and godliness in all conversation (Matt 5:33–37; James 5:12), but there is no parallel for the Old Testament death penalty. It must be concluded that the third Mosaic law has been done away but it must be recognized that the principle upon which it was based is as timeless as the holiness of God.

The Mosaic Law was specific about Saturday: "Remember the sabbath day, to keep it holy." It went on to stipulate: "Six days you shall labor and do all your work, but the seventh day is a sabbath of the LORD your God; in it you shall not do any work, you or your son or your daughter, your male or your female servant or your cattle or your sojourner who stays with you."

We find no such command and no restatement or even suggestion of keeping the Sabbath in the New Testament. In Colossians 2:14–17, Paul specifically singles out this command and says that the cross of Christ cancelled it. We see the unrelenting harshness and burden of the Mosaic Law in the enforcement of its penalty in the case of the man found gathering sticks on the Sabbath, who was stoned to death by the explicit instruction of the Lord (Numbers 15:32–36). The Sabbath was the sign of the Mosaic Law, but since the Mosaic Law has been annulled, it would stand to reason that its sign would be abolished as well.

Excursus: Sunday

When we look at church history, we see that Sunday worship was a universal practice of all churches outside of Israel by the beginning of the second century (*cf. From Sabbath to Lord's Day* (Carson, 2001)). However, Sunday was never, in those early days, considered "the Sabbath." Over the course of time, though, Sabbath practices were imported into Sunday worship, and Sabbath rules were applied to Sunday ... and that has continued until today.

In the Puritan communities of colonial America, Sabbath rules infected Sunday. According to the *Encyclopedia Britannica,*

> Sunday laws usually forbade regular work on that day, plus any buying, selling, traveling, public entertainment, or sports ... To some degree, similar laws existed in all the American colonies. ... [Sunday laws], especially those regarding the sale of alcohol, remained on the statutes in some states into the 21st century, and their influence persisted wherever public activity on Sunday was regulated.

There is no such thing as a "Christian Sabbath," as some call it. To use such nomenclature is to import law into grace; those who do so do not recognize that the New Testament never refers to Sunday as the Sabbath; it's always called "the first day of the week."

At this point even dispensationalists become inconsistent: Dr. Merrill F. Unger, in his *Bible Dictionary* (1964), writes, "In the present dispensation of grace, Sunday perpetuates the truth that one-seventh of one's time belongs to God."

It's a fact that the early church met on Sunday, but this does not mean that believers are commanded to meet on that day. In the dispensation of Grace, we are free and not under any obligation to set aside a particular day for worship. Each church would therefore be free to choose whichever day it desires. It is not wrong to meet on Sunday, but it's not mandatory either (Fruchtenbaum, 2001).

Because of a strong tradition, we tend to think that it's mandatory for a church to meet on Sunday morning. But in Acts 20:5–7, we see that the church at Troas met on Saturday night because, for the Jews, the first day of the week began at sundown on Saturday, not at 12:01 on Sunday morning. The church at Troas didn't meet on Sunday morning, they met on Saturday night, which, according to their reckoning of time, was the beginning of Sunday, the first day of the week. This was the incident when Paul preached until midnight. This text would make no sense if we assumed that the church met at 11:00 a.m. on Sunday morning; that would mean that Paul preached for thirteen hours, from 11:00 a.m. until midnight on Sunday. That would be a pauline filibuster!

To understand that, in the Grace Dispensation, a local church is free to meet on any day it chooses would solve an annual problem for American churches when the Super Bowl arrives. Those churches which hold that they *must* meet on Sunday night find their pews bare and attendance embarrassingly meager. (After all, particularly in the South, football is a religion.) Many churches try to solve the problem by gathering to watch the big game on giant TV screens and then, at halftime, have their "service," rendering the benediction just before the second half kickoff. It apparently never occurs to them either to cancel the service or to meet on Saturday evening (or Thursday night, or Wednesday morning), either of which they are free to do, but they don't consider it because Sunday-go-to-meeting is ingrained in thought and tradition as being obligatory.

Back to the Ten Commandments

The fifth commandment says: "Honor your father and your mother, that your days may be prolonged in the land which the LORD your God gives you." Violation of this command carried the death penalty (Exodus 21:15, 21:17; Deuteronomy 21:18–21, 27:16a).

Jesus repeated this commandment in Matthew 15:3 4: "And He answered and said to them, 'Why do you yourselves transgress the commandment of God for the sake of your tradition? For God said, 'Honor your father and mother,' and, 'He who speaks evil of father or mother is to be put to death.'" Jesus lived under the Mosaic Law as an obedient Jew; His birth didn't end the Law, His death did (Colossians 2:14). When He quoted the command, He was speaking to the Pharisees and the scribes who were also Jews living during the Dispensation of the Law.

There are those who point to Ephesians 6:1–3 as proof positive that the Mosaic Law is binding on the believer: "Children, obey your parents in the Lord, for this is right. Honor your father and mother (which is the first commandment with a promise), so that it may be well with you, and that you may live long on the earth." Yet, it's interesting that the same ones who quote this Ephesians text ignore Jesus' statement in Matthew 15. The reason they do so is simple: they want to avoid the capital punishment clause of the command. We must remember that a law without a penalty is no law at all.

Roy L. Aldrich (1961) points out that "Christ recognized that this law [the fifth commandment] as Mosaic legislation could not be separated from its death penalty. But in Ephesians the penalty is omitted and nowhere is it reinstated for this age of grace. It should also be noted that the promise of long life in the land of Palestine as a reward for obedience is changed to a promise of long life on the earth—thus making the reward of universal application for the new age" (p. 254).

It's important to note that the nine commandments that are repeated in principle, but without their Mosaic Law penalties, are carried over into the Grace Dispensation and thereby made compatible with the dispensation in which we live: that is, they are synchronizing with grace. Although incorporated into the Law of

Christ, we recognize that the Law of Moses and the Law of Christ are two separate systems. If believers are under the Mosaic Law (which they are not), they are under the penalties that go along with the Mosaic Law. The one cannot be separated from the other. To make such a separation is arbitrary and inconsistent.

> **The Law of Moses and the Law of Christ are two separate systems.**

The sixth commandment states: "You shall not murder." With this command, we see dispensationally what God is doing. By the time we come to the Grace Dispensation, there are certain commands that have been retained, and certain commands that have not been included in the Law of Christ (for example, Sabbath observance and diet). This sixth commandment was in effect beginning with the Noahic Covenant (Genesis 9:5–6) and from there was incorporated into the Mosaic Law for Israel. The gentile world remains under the Noahic Covenant, and Israel was under the Mosaic Law, but the believer is under the Law of Christ, which expands this law to say that hatred is the beginning of murder in that the hater has found someone whom he wishes would drop off the face of the earth (1 John 3:15).

The seventh commandment safeguarded marriage and the family in Israel: "You shall not commit adultery." The legislation regarding this commandment also exacted the death penalty as the punishment. Although the Law of Christ forbids adultery, it does not call for the death penalty; instead, it calls for the removal of the unrepentant believer from the fellowship of the church so that he might come to his senses and be restored.

"You shall not steal" is the eighth commandment. This commandment carries the penalty of restoring to the victim four and sometimes fivefold what was stolen (Exodus 22:1). However, kidnapping (the stealing of a person) was punishable by death under the Mosaic Law (Exodus 21:16).

In Ephesians 4:28, we see this law incorporated into the Law of Christ without the four- and fivefold penalty: "He who steals must steal no longer; but rather he must labor, performing with his own hands what is good, so that he will have *something* to share with one who has need." This text instructs the believer to go to work instead of stealing, with the added provision that when he does, not only is he to support himself, but also to share with others. Thus, under grace, this negative command of the Mosaic Law becomes a principle of stewardship.

The next-to-last of the Ten Commandments deals with stealing someone's reputation: "You shall not bear false witness against your neighbor." If an Israelite gave false testimony in a murder case, the penalty for murder was exacted for his perjury. But in the Law of Christ, this command is restated in line with grace: "Do not lie to one another, since you laid aside the old self with its *evil* practices, and have put on the new self who is being renewed to a true knowledge according to the image of the One who created him" (Colossians 3:9–10). The reason for honesty in the Law of Christ is because it's consistent with our new nature in Christ; under the Mosaic Law, the appeal to honesty was based on the fear of punishment.

And so, we come to the last of the Ten: "You shall not covet your neighbor's house; you shall not covet your neighbor's wife or his male servant or his female servant or his ox or his donkey or anything that belongs to your neighbor." This command is unique among the Ten in that it's a thought crime, and we notice that there is no penalty attached—none whatsoever. Of course, coveting often leads to overt crimes such as stealing and adultery, which do carry penalties.

The Law of Christ stipulates this command in Ephesians 5:3: "But immorality or any impurity or greed must not even be named among you, as is proper among saints." Here we see yet again that the appeal to keeping this command of the Law of Christ is based on what is proper for the believer's position in Christ, not on the fear of the Mosaic Law with its penalties. This is what is meant in the summary statement that all but one of the Ten Commandments are carried over into the Law of Christ, and are carried over according to the principles of grace.

What This Shows Us

In reviewing the penalties of the Mosaic Law, we can understand more clearly why Paul called the Ten Commandments "the ministry of death, in letters engraved on stones" (2 Corinthians 3:7). There are those who charge the dispensationalist with antinomianism, "the belief that Christians are freed from the moral law by virtue of grace as set forth in the gospel" (*Random House Dictionary*, 2017). But, seriously, how can such a charge be made? As Aldrich (1961) writes: "[The Christian] is under all the moral principles of those stones restated appropriately for the economy of grace. He is under the eternal moral law of God which demands far more than the Ten Commandments. It calls for nothing less than conformity to the character of God."

The Christian must realize his freedom from the condemnation of the Mosaic Law and live free of it. Arnold Fruchtenbaum (2001) summarizes it well: "If we [believers of the Grace Dispensation] do not kill or steal today, this is not because of the Law of Moses but because of the Law of Christ. On the other hand, if I steal, I am not guilty of breaking the Law of Moses but of breaking the Law of Christ."

The Law in Church History

There is no more important doctrine in Christianity than its teaching that forgiveness of sin and eternal life come not from the Mosaic Law, but from *faith alone in Christ alone*. In the first century and thereafter, rabbinic Judaism stood ramrod straight with the Pharisees to oppose that doctrine. Jesus faced their hostility, as did Paul and the other apostles.

After the era of the apostles, the Church Fathers also faced opposition from the rabbis; rabbinic literature was filled with salvation by works. Irvin A. Busenitz (2005) writes,

> The rabbis taught that mankind could, by some means, acquire merit with God by personal efforts. A rabbinical account, dated at the end of the first century A.D., relates, "When R[abbi] Eliezer fell ill, his disciples went in to visit him. They said to him, "Master, teach us the paths of life so that we may through them win the life of the future world."

> He said to them: "Be solicitous for the honor of your colleagues, and keep your children from meditation, and set them between the knees of scholars, and when you pray, know before whom you are standing and in this way you will win the future world."

The Church Fathers are the early and influential theologians and writers in the Christian church, particularly those of the first five centuries of the Christian era. "Church Fathers" refers specifically to the writers and teachers of the church. They wrote about the Law, salvation, and justification. The following is a summary of their writings based mostly on the research of Irvin A. Busenitz.

Ignatius of Antioch (37–107 AD)
While we would condemn Ignatius's hatred of the Jews (he called them "agents of the evil one"), he did draw a clear line of demarcation between the Law Dispensation and the Dispensation of Grace when he wrote a letter to the Magnesian church in which he said, "It is outrageous to utter the name of Jesus Christ and live in Judaism." In the same letter, he referred to Judaism as "an antiquated, legalistic faith based on nothing now the Messiah has come and the former *'people of God'* have rejected him."

Ignatius advised the church: "Be not deceived with strange doctrines, 'nor give heed to fables and endless genealogies,' and things in which the Jews make their boast. 'Old things are passed away: behold, all things have become new.' For if we still live according to the Jewish law, and the circumcision of the flesh, we deny that we have received grace."

He noted that Christians no longer observed the Sabbath, but were "living in the observance of the Lord's Day ... For where there is Christianity there cannot be Judaism."

Clement of Rome (First Century AD)
There are those who believe that Clement of Rome is the Clement Paul mentioned in Philippians 4:3, but that's highly debatable. However, there is evidence that Clement knew and had interaction with Peter and studied under the apostles. We know this from Irenaeus (130–200 AD) who wrote, "This man [Clement of Rome], as he had seen the blessed apostles, and had been conversant with them, might be said to have the preaching of the apostles still echoing [in his ears], and their traditions before his eyes" (*Against Heresies*, 3:3).

Clement of Rome was an elder in the late first century AD. The Roman Catholics call him a pope (Pope Clement I), but his letter is one of the best pieces of evidence against the existence of a pope in the early second century (see Pavao, n.d.).

In Clement's *Epistle to the Corinthians* (96 AD), Clement wrote about trying to gain salvation by works, saying that they make no contribution to one's justification: "We, therefore, who have been called by His will in Christ Jesus, are not justified by ourselves, neither by our wisdom or understanding or piety, nor by the works we have wrought in holiness of heart, but by the faith by which almighty God has justified all men from the beginning."

Tertullian (ca. 155/160–after 220 AD)

Tertullian was born in Carthage, North Africa, the city infamous for being the ancient enemy of Rome. When he was converted to Christianity in mid-life, he left the study of law to study theology.

Tertullian argues that "man might be justified by the liberty of faith, not by servitude to the law, 'because the just shall live by his faith.' Now, although the prophet Habakkuk first said this, yet you have the apostle [Paul] here confirming the prophets, even as Christ did. The object, therefore, of the faith whereby the just man shall live, will be that same God to whom likewise belongs the law, by doing which no man is justified" (n.d.).

Chrysostom (ca. 347–407 AD)

Despite being born into wealth, John Chrysostom would forgo the pleasures of the world, living a simple life in the study of Scripture and preaching. Chrysostom was "recognized in his sober exegesis, occupied with determining the literal sense of his text" (Preuschen, 1900).

His sermons covered almost every book in the Bible and in some of those homilies he wrote of his understanding of Paul and the Law. When he commented on Romans 1:17, he said that one's righteousness is "not thine own, but that of God... For you do not achieve it by toilings and labors, but you receive it by a gift from above, contributing one thing only from your own store, believing."

In his sermon on Romans 3:31, he argues that good works are the result of justification by grace: "But since after this grace, whereby we were justified, there is need also of a life suited to it, let us show an earnestness worthy of the gift." In his explanation of Romans 4:1ff, he noted that Paul argues that it was impossible to be saved other than by faith. He asks his listeners to meditate upon how "great a thing it is to be persuaded and have full confidence that God is able on a sudden not to free a man who has lived in impiety from punishment only, but even to make him just, and to count him worthy of those immortal honors."

Justin Martyr (100–165 AD)

Justin Martyr was a trained, professional philosopher and a prolific writer, with three of his books surviving today. One of his works is "Dialogue with the Jew Trypho." In chapter 27 of that book, Justin writes of a conversation between himself and Trypho in which Justin explains to Trypho that some weak-minded people may believe there is some virtue in observing the Mosaic legislation and who may thus wish to keep that Law while exercising faith in Christ. These, according to Justin, are saved individuals and therefore should be fellowshipped with. His references to circumcision, the Sabbath, and other observances, and the prohibition against efforts to draw gentiles into this dual observance of Law and faith in Christ, make it clear that Jews are being spoken of here. But Justin added that those Jews who confess faith in Christ and then turn back completely to the "legal dispensation," and "those of the seed of Abraham who live according to the Law" and "do anathematize this very Christ in the synagogues," are totally without hope of salvation.

His references to those Jews who "turn back completely to the legal dispensation" as those who "anathematize this very Christ in the synagogues" show his belief that a new dispensation has come; there is to be no turning back to the Mosaic Law. He was right on.

Yet, the same Justin Martyr wrote: "Those who are found not living as he [Jesus] taught should know that they are not really Christians, even if his teachings are on their lips, for he said that not those who merely profess but those who also do the works will be saved." He also noted, "Each man goes to everlasting punishment or salvation according to the value of his actions" and "[t]he matters of our religion lie in works, not in words."

It is as if Justin Martyr, among other Church Fathers, rightly turned from the Law as the way of salvation, but then instituted their own "law." For example, Justin, in his Dialogue, wrote: "Those who are convinced of the truth of our doctrine ... are exhorted to prayer, fasting and repentance for past sins; ... Then they are led by us to a place where there is water, and in this way they are regenerated, as we also have been regenerated; ... For Christ says: 'Except you are born again, you cannot enter into the kingdom of heaven.'" He went on to say about baptism: "The laver of repentance ... is baptism, the only thing which is able to cleanse those who have repented."

Irenaeus (ca. 120–202 AD)

Irenaeus was a third-generation Christian. He was a student of a student of the Apostle John named Polycarp. He was an apologist and theologian who wrote *Against Heresies* (ca. 180 AD). As one of the first Christian theologians, he emphasized the Scriptures and tradition.

Irenaeus describes his memories of Polycarp:

> I remember the events of that time more clearly than those of recent years. For what boys learn, growing with their mind, becomes joined with it; so that I am able to describe the very place in which the blessed Polycarp sat as he discoursed, and his goings out and his comings in, and the manner of his life, and his physical appearance, and his discourses to the people, and the accounts which he gave of his intercourse

with John and with the others who had seen the Lord. And as he remembered their words, and what he heard from them concerning the Lord, and concerning his miracles and his teaching, having received them from eyewitnesses of the "Word of life," Polycarp related all things in harmony with the Scriptures.

Irenaeus wrote about the Mosaic Law, saying, "The ancient Law has been abolished, we freely admit, and hold that it actually proceeds from the dispensation of the Creator...." He went on to teach, "Now, if the Creator indeed promised that the ancient things should pass away to be superseded by a new course of things which should arise, whilst Christ marks the period of the separation when He says, 'The law and prophets were until John;—thus marking the Baptist the limit between the two dispensations of the old things then terminating and the new things then beginning, the apostle cannot of course do otherwise...." Writing about the book of Galatians, Irenaeus said: "Therefore the purport of this epistle is simply to show us that the supersession [the state of being superseded] of the law comes from the appointment of the Creator—a point which we shall still have to keep in mind."

Irenaeus wrote about the abolition of the Law. He explained that the former covenant, the legal dispensation, resulted in bondage. But, as he recognized, the new covenant under Christ—the greater of the two dispensations—brought forth liberty and multiplied grace (Irenaeus, IV, IX, 1–2). Yet, the same Irenaeus wrote: "But to the righteous and holy, and those *who have kept his commandments* and have remained in his love...he will by his grace give life incorrupt, and will clothe them with eternal glory" [italics added].

Larry V. Crutchfield summarizes the early Church Fathers' stance regarding their theology of Israel and the church which bears upon the question of their belief concerning the Mosaic Law and its imposition on the church: "The Fathers distinguished between the church and national Israel ... The contemporary dispensational position on Israel and the church is primarily a refinement and not a contradiction of the position of the ante-Nicene church" (Crutchfield, 1987b; see also Crutchfield, 1987a).

Augustine (354–430 AD)

Augustine was born near Carthage. His father was a pagan who worshipped the old Punic gods, which would have included Baal, Asherah, and Mot, the god of the dead. In his early years, Augustine loved to criticize the Old Testament, ridiculing the ordinances of the church and often debating Christians. At age 18, he took a concubine whose name he never mentioned and they had a child whom they called Adeodatus — "a gift from God."

During this time, Augustine's mother continued to pray for her promiscuous son, petitioning the Lord for his salvation. In his early thirties, he did become a convert to Christianity after living life as a dissolute heathen in the fullest sense of the word. He then turned his intellect and extensive education toward writing a defense of the faith.

Augustine was clear concerning first-century Judaism. He explained Romans 3:20: "The law brings the knowledge, not the overcoming, of sin." Concerning Romans 9:31–32, Augustine taught that the text indicates that Israel thought they could establish their own righteousness, but could not. However, Augustine brought a boatload of erroneous theology into the church because he, in contrast to Luther, came to believe that justification was a lifelong effort, whereas Luther knew that justification was a declaration of God, whereby the sinner is *declared* righteous, not *made* righteous.

Augustine erroneously believed that at the regeneration of baptism, Christ's character was infused into the believer (most commonly at the baptism of infants) and that this character would remain until death, and then and only then would the person be made righteous enough "to get in."

Augustine invested all his soteriological marbles on one verse. It is neither John 3:16 nor Ephesians 2:8–9. His primary text, which he quoted more than those two verses, was Matthew 24:13: "But he who endures to the end shall be saved." Unfortunately, Augustine ripped the verse from its context of enduring until "the end of the age," which is a clear reference to physically enduring until the end of the Great Tribulation and being delivered physically from that worst time in world history. Instead, Augustine understood "saved" as referring to spiritual salvation, not to a physical deliverance from the clutches of the antiChrist after the rapture of the church.

This reading and conclusion forced him into a position of having no assurance of salvation for himself or for anyone else. Who can possibly know if he will persevere faithful to Christ until the end of his life, no matter how faithful he may be today? After all, a person can fall away and make a shipwreck of the faith, in which case the wrecked life proves that the person was never saved in the first place, according to the reasoning of those holding Augustine's position. Augustine wrote: "Therefore it is uncertain whether anyone has received this gift so long as he is still alive. For if he fall before he dies, he is, of course, said not to have persevered; and most truly is it said, How then should he be said to have received or to have perseverance who has not persevered?"

This belief about salvation led to believers trying to live lives of asceticism and self-denial, so as to ensure perseverance by keeping themselves on the straight and narrow and away from the primrose path. By this interpretation, self-denial is a *sine qua non* for salvation. Asceticism 101 becomes a required course to enter heaven. Augustine said, "Self-denial of all sorts if one perseveres to the end of his life, will bring salvation." Going even farther,

Augustine said, "If one loves his wife, parents, or children more than Christ, he is not elect."

There is only one conclusion we can draw from the words of Augustine: "this kind of 'self-denial salvation' is none other than a works approach to eternal life" (Dr. David R. Anderson, 2010). Augustine saw this difficulty and tried to solve it by citing Philippians 2:12–13, saying that perseverance is a grace gift from God, since God is the One who gives the regenerated and baptized believer the power to persevere. But, as Dr. Anderson points out, this does not solve the problem, it only raises an unanswerable one: "Why is it that God gives some baptized regenerate believers the gift of perseverance to the end, but does not give it to others?" "It's a mystery," replies Augustine. This is the pattern of Calvinism today: when inconsistencies in their system show up, they call them "mysteries." It would be better to call them "contradictions."

Augustine is the one in church history to whom we must attribute limited atonement (Christ died only for the elect) and double predestination (God chose some to go to heaven and God chose the rest to go to hell before anyone was created). It was also Augustine who invented the idea of the baptismal regeneration of infants. Based on his misunderstanding of Romans 5:12, Augustine, going against more than three hundred years of orthodox teaching, believed that every baby is worthy of being sent to hell. In Augustine's theology, this necessitated infant baptism which would "be the laver of regeneration" that would wash away the guilt of sin and simultaneously regenerate the newly born. In this context, one must wonder about Numbers 32:11: "None of the men who came up from Egypt, from twenty years old and upward, shall see the land which I swore to Abraham, to Isaac and to Jacob; for they did not follow Me fully...." Those Israelites, up until age 19, were not held accountable for Israel's rebellion in the wilderness.

It was church historian Philip Schaff who wrote that the subject of the saving work of Christ in the hands of Augustine is both gloomy and full of contradictions (1999). That is what we would expect when one departs from salvation by grace.

A Mixed Bag

The Church Fathers did recognize that the Law was over and abolished as a rule of life for the believer, yet they still imported works into salvation. Polycarp (69–156 AD) wrote, "Now He that raised Him from the dead will raise us also; if we do His will and walk in His commandments and love the things which He loved, abstaining from all unrighteousness, covetousness, love of money, evil speaking, false witness; not rendering evil for evil or railing for railing or blow for blow or cursing for cursing …." Polycarp's to-do list for salvation speaks of "abstaining from all unrighteousness." But has any member of the fallen human race achieved this at any time anywhere in human history? Of course not, not even the very best Christian you know (1 John 1:8–10).

Remember Clement of Rome? He wrote:

> And we, too, being called by His will in Christ Jesus, are not justified by ourselves, nor by our own wisdom, or understanding, or godliness, or works which we have wrought in holiness of heart; but by that faith through which, from the beginning, Almighty God has justified all men; to whom be glory, glory for ever and ever. Amen.

Then Clement wrote, just two very short chapters later: "Let us clothe ourselves with concord and humility, ever exercising self-control, standing far off from all whispering and evil-speaking, being justified by our works, and not our words. … If we do the will of Christ, we shall obtain rest; but if not, if we neglect his commandments, nothing will rescue us from eternal punishment."

Say what? In one statement he says, we are saved "by that faith through which ... Almighty God has justified all men," and then he writes of "being justified by our works, and not our words."

What's happening is that Clement of Rome nowhere speaks of justification by faith *alone*, and this is in complete agreement with the Council of Trent, which began meeting on December 13, 1545. The meeting was the response of the Roman Catholic Church to the Reformation. This official conclave declared that salvation is not by faith alone, instead saying that we are justified by faith *and* works, that works contribute to our justification. The Council's viewpoint was that justification is not a definitive act; it's a process. In Canon 9, the Council said: "If anyone says that the sinner is justified by faith alone, meaning that nothing else is required to cooperate in order to obtain the grace of justification and that it is not in any way necessary that he be prepared and disposed by the action of his own will, let him be anathema" (*anathema* means "excommunicated"; Merriam-Webster.com, 2020).

Yet, the Bible stands solidly against Canon 9:

- "because by the works of the Law no flesh will be justified in His sight; for through the Law comes the knowledge of sin" (Romans 3:20).

- "being justified as a gift by His grace through the redemption which is in Christ Jesus" (Romans 3:24).

- "For we maintain that a man is justified by faith apart from works of the Law" (Romans 3:28).

- "For what does the Scripture say? 'Abraham believed God, and it was credited to him as righteousness'" (Romans 4:3).

- "Therefore, having been justified by faith, we have peace with God through our Lord Jesus Christ" (Romans 5:1).

- "For by grace you have been saved through faith; and that not of yourselves, it is the gift of God" (Ephesians 2:8).

- "He saved us, not on the basis of deeds which we have done in righteousness, but according to His mercy, by the washing of regeneration and renewing by the Holy Spirit" (Titus 3:5).

In Canon 12, the Council said: "If any one saith, that justifying faith is nothing else but confidence in the divine mercy which remits sins for Christ's sake; or, that this confidence alone is that whereby we are justified; let him be anathema." But Paul, John, and the author of Hebrews disagree:

- "But as many as received Him, to them He gave the right to become children of God, even to those who believe in His name" (John 1:12).

- "For we maintain that a man is justified by faith apart from works of the Law" (Romans 3:28).

- "For what does the Scripture say? "Abraham believed God, and it was credited to him as righteousness"" (Romans 4:3).

- "Therefore He is able also to save forever those who draw near to God through Him, since He always lives to make intercession for them. 26 For it was fitting for us to have such a high priest, holy, innocent, undefiled, separated from sinners and exalted above the heavens; 27 who does not need daily, like those high priests, to offer up sacrifices, first for His own sins and then for the sins of the people, because this He did once for all when He offered up Himself" (Hebrews 7:25–27).

- "For this reason I also suffer these things, but I am not ashamed; for I know whom I have believed and I am convinced that He is able to guard what I have entrusted to Him until that day" (2 Timothy 1:12).

Not content with Canons 9 and 12, the Council continued in Canon 14: "If any one saith, that man is truly absolved from his sins and justified, because that he assuredly believed himself absolved and justified; or, that no one is truly justified but he who believes himself justified; and that, by this faith alone, absolution and justification are effected; let him be anathema." The book of Romans answers:

- "For what does the Scripture say? 'Abraham believed God, and it was credited to him as righteousness'" (Romans 4:3).

- "Therefore, having been justified by faith, we have peace with God through our Lord Jesus Christ" (Romans 5:1).

The Coming Home Network, an outreach of modern-day Roman Catholicism, shows that the Council of Trent has never been repudiated. Chris Erickson of The Coming Home Network wrote in 2010,

> Clement taught that the Christian moral life is imperative for salvation, that faith and obedience are what God considers necessary for the process of being made righteous. Clement points out that our actions—our good deeds prompted by faith—are what God reckons as righteousness: "Why was our father Abraham blessed? Was it not because he *acted in righteousness* and truth, *prompted by faith*?" Clement further instructed the Church of Corinth that Abraham inherited God's promises because of his (1) faith, (2) obedience and (3) hospitality...

Today

The Coming Home Network turns approvingly to Ignatius of Antioch (35–107 AD) for the following testimony:

> [Ignatius] says that along with baptism, faith and charity, our works will be our deposits to receive what is our due:

Let your baptism be ever your shield, your faith a helmet, your charity a spear, your patience a panoply. Let your works be deposits, so that you may receive the sum that is due you" (Letter to St. Polycarp, 6).

Is Ignatius telling us that we are *due* something from God? Our due is death as a result of sin. But what is our due after baptism, faith, charity, and obedience to God's will? Then, we are due God's promises *according to the conditions God set forth*. Thus spoke Ignatius.

What Ignatius tells us is a complete destruction of grace, because he considers salvation to be what is due us after being baptized and obedient according to the conditions (plural) of salvation He set forth. This is the corruption of salvation as a free gift into wages owed as payment for work.

What Paul wrote in Romans 4:4–5 opposes such nonsense: "Now to the one who works, his wage is not credited as a favor, but as what is due. But to the one who does not work, but believes in Him who justifies the ungodly, his faith is credited as righteousness."

Missing It by a Mile

How could these men, living during or so close to the time of the apostles, miss it? How could they be so wrong and misunderstand the doctrine and meaning of grace? When we ask such a question, we're reading the present time back into the early days of the church. Their day was not as ours is. The completed canon of Scripture today is ubiquitous in America. According to a 2015 survey, the vast majority of households in America (88%) own at least one Bible and many own more than one (Barna Group, 2015). That was not the case in their world.

Thomas Torrence (1996) points out that back in the early decades of the church age, Paul's epistles weren't in general circulation.

It was not until approximately 110 AD that his letters became widespread. Because of that, the Old Testament was the Christian's book and its impact was powerful; therefore, the Mosaic Law had a great influence on the Church Fathers and a striving after righteousness infected their outlook — the same viewpoint that exists today.

In addition, the Church Fathers' definition of *grace* is what we find in current circulation today. Whenever I talk to people about the gospel, I'm very interested to learn their definition of grace. When I ask, "What does the word 'grace' mean to you," most can give no answer, even if they've been sitting in church, hearing the sermons, and singing "Amazing Grace" all their lives.

I probe further: "Have you heard of the word?"

"Oh, yes," they answer, "all the time in church."

"But you don't know what it means?"

"No," is a common response.

Assuming knowledge is a dangerous thing.

Many, when pressed for an answer as to the meaning of *grace*, define it as an inner or outer attractiveness, such as we find in an Olympic figure skater or an accomplished ballroom dancer. This was the way the Greek mind in the ancient world would have defined grace, along with the idea that grace involved a reward for a favor, like our word "gratuity." By such a definition, the Church Fathers negated the Bible's definition of grace as undeserved, unmerited favor. Therefore, when the Church Fathers read, "The grace of our Lord Jesus Christ," they read it as "the attractiveness of our Lord Jesus Christ," just as people do today.

When we ask, "How could those living in the same time people as the apostles, or nearly so, have missed it?" we also have to recognize that even *while* the apostles were alive and teaching, there were those who misunderstood, twisted, distorted, and rejected their teaching. We see this in Acts 8, Acts 15, the book of Galatians, and 2 Peter 3:16.

Moving On in Church History

Aquinas (1225–1274 AD)

Thomas Aquinas, born in Italy, began his studies in a Dominican monastery, finishing his education in Cologne, Germany, with Albertus Magnus, a well-known philosopher who introduced Aquinas to the Greek philosophers. As a student, Thomas Aquinas was reserved and not liked by his colleagues. Physically, Aquinas was stout and large, which caused his fellow students to give him the nickname of "the dumb Sicilian Ox." However, his professor responded, "We call Brother Thomas the 'Dumb Ox'; but I tell you that he will yet make his lowing heard to the uttermost parts of the earth."

Professor Albertus was correct in his estimation of his most famous student. According to many scholars, from the Middle Ages until the present, Aquinas has influenced the Roman Catholic Church more than any other person. Aquinas's *magnum opus*, the *Summa Theologica* (a five-volume set), is still in print today. He believed in the concept of justification by grace and, believing that this justification includes the remission of sins, he also held that the sacraments were efficacious. He taught that Christians receive an infusion of grace at baptism that remains within the soul. In addition, he attempted to salvage the political wisdom of the Old Testament by arguing that the Mosaic Law can still serve as a guide for Christian political thinkers.

Martin Luther (1483–1546)

In the sixteenth century, the world was divided about Martin Luther. One Catholic thought Martin Luther was a "demon in the appearance of a man." Another, who at first questioned

Luther's theology, later declared, "He alone is right!" No matter one's opinion, Martin Luther, the monk once terrified of the wrath of God, changed the course of history ("Christian History").

As John H. Armstrong (1998) wrote, "Martin Luther was the human torch that lit the fire of the Protestant revolt against the Church of Rome in the sixteenth century. And the fire he lit has never gone out, now nearly five centuries later."

But prior to becoming the "torch that lit the fire," Luther was a dark and tortured soul, living as a monk in an Augustinian monastery; he was terrified of the wrath of God and unsure of his salvation. As a monk, striving for heaven, he plunged into prayer, forced himself into fasting, and endured rigorous ascetic practices. He denied himself sleep; when he did sleep, it was without the benefit of a blanket in bone- and flesh-numbing cold, and, if that were not enough, he put the whip to his back. He was so scared of God that he went to confession as many as 10 times a day. He later commented, "If anyone could have earned heaven by the life of a monk, it was I."

Luther's self-inflicted tortures prompt questions: How many lashes are enough? How many hours of sleep deprivation are enough? How many meals must be missed? How many hours of prayer are enough? How many confessions a day are enough? If one says, "Thirty-nine lashes are enough," why not 40? If it's 20 missed meals, why not 21? No wonder Luther was afraid.

Then it happened: he came to understand that justification was not something he was to earn. He said, "At last, meditating day and night, by the mercy of God, I began to understand that the righteousness of God is that through which the righteous live by a gift of God, namely by faith. Here I felt as if I were entirely born again and had entered paradise itself through the gates that had been flung open."

When Luther walked through those gates of his new-found Paradise, he saw other truths:

> On the heels of this new understanding came others.... Salvation came not by the sacraments as such but by faith. The idea that human beings had a spark of goodness (enough to seek out God) was not a foundation of theology but was taught only by "fools." Humility was no longer a virtue that earned grace but a necessary response to the gift of grace. Faith no longer consisted of assenting to the church's teachings but of trusting the promises of God and the merits of Christ. ("Christian History")

In regard to faith, Luther defined *saving faith* as "the sort of faith which does not look at its own strength and worthiness, noting what sort of quality or new created or infused virtue it may be ... But faith goes out of itself, clings to Christ, and embraces Him as its own possession; and faith is certain it is loved by God for its own sake."

Luther's vocabulary describing his opposition to the Pope and Roman Catholicism is a force in and of itself. He expressed the truth with verbal claps of thunder and bolts of lightning, as we see in his descriptions of the Mosaic Law. Luther called the Law God's "great hammer" which He used to drive humanity to complete despair and to show humankind its need for the Savior. Luther said, "The Law is the hammer of death, the thundering of hell and the lightning of God's wrath, that beats to powder the obstinate and senseless hypocrites. Wherefore this is the proper and absolute use of the law, ... to beat down and rend in pieces that beast which is called the opinion of righteousness ... To Luther, this was the main reason for the Law."

Justification by faith was crucial in Luther's view. He said that without the doctrine of justification, "the church of God is not able to exist for one hour." Luther viewed Galatians 2:16 as the peak of Mount Everest of Paul's view of the saving work of God: "[N]evertheless, knowing that a man is not justified by the works of the Law but through faith in Christ Jesus, even we have believed in Christ Jesus, so that we may be justified by faith in Christ and not by the works of the Law; since by the works of the Law no flesh will be justified."

When he explained Galatians 2:16, his words were crystal clear and to the point:

> The Law is a good thing. But when the discussion is about justification, then is no time to drag in the Law. When we discuss justification we ought to speak of Christ and the benefits He has brought us. Christ is no sheriff. He is "the Lamb of God, which taketh away the sin of the world" (John 1:29). We must know that we are nothing. We must understand that we are merely beneficiaries and recipients of the treasures of Christ.

However, Luther did not see the Law as given only to Israel; he believed that it was given to all mankind to govern civil life in general. Sadly, Martin Luther wrote the Ten Commandments into his Small Catechism with a brief explanation of each. In a short introduction, he counseled obedience to them: "God threatens to punish all who transgress these commandments. Therefore we should fear his anger and not disobey what he commands. But he promises grace and every blessing to all who keep these commandments. Therefore we should love and trust in him, and gladly obey what he commands."

Under the commandment to "Remember the Sabbath day by keeping it holy," Luther asked, "What does this mean?" He explained, "We should fear and love God that we do not despise preaching and his Word, but regard it as holy, and gladly hear and learn it." That's good advice, but is that what the commandment says?

In the Large Catechism, Luther states his "Conclusion of the Ten Commandments" as translated by F. Bente and W. H. T. Dau (1921):

> This (I say) it is profitable and necessary always to teach to the young people, to admonish them and to remind them of it, that they may be brought up not only with blows and compulsion, like cattle, but in the fear and reverence of God. For where this is considered and laid to heart that these things are not human trifles, but the commandments of the Divine Majesty, who insists upon them with such earnestness, is angry with, and punishes those who despise them, and, on the other hand, abundantly rewards those who keep them, there will be a spontaneous impulse and a desire gladly to do the will of God.

> Therefore it is not in vain that it is commanded in the Old Testament to write the Ten Commandments on all walls and corners, yes, even on the garments, not for the sake of merely having them written in these places and making a show of them, as did the Jews, but that we might have our eyes constantly fixed upon them, and have them always in our memory, and that we might practise them in all our actions and ways, and every one make them his daily exercise in all cases, in every business and transaction, as though they were written in every place wherever he would look, yea, wherever he walks or stands. Thus there would be occasion enough, both at home in our own house and abroad with our neighbors, to practise the Ten Commandments, that no one need run far for them.

> From this it again appears how highly these Ten Commandments are to be exalted and extolled above all estates, commandments, and works which are taught and practised aside from them. For here we can boast and say:

Let all the wise and saints step forth and produce, if they can, a [single] work like these commandments, upon which God insists with such earnestness, and which He enjoins with His greatest wrath and punishment, and, besides, adds such glorious promises that He will pour out upon us all good things and blessings. Therefore they should be taught above all others, and be esteemed precious and dear, as the highest treasure given by God.

Donald Grey Barnhouse wrote: "It was a tragic hour when the Reformation churches wrote the Ten Commandments into their creeds and catechisms and sought to bring Gentile believers into bondage to Jewish law, which was never intended either for the Gentile nations or for the church" (cited in deMar, 2020).

John Calvin (1509–1564)

There were those who believed Calvin to be a child prodigy; when he was 12, he became a chaplain at his home-town cathedral. When he was 19, he began to study for a law degree and, having come under the influence of humanism, he abandoned that to study the humanities.

In personality, Calvin was more taciturn than his contemporary Martin Luther. Calvin visualized his ideal life as being one of solitude, study, and writing. He wrote about the Mosaic Law saying that it was given to Moses on Mount Sinai, in contrast with the gospel of God's grace. Along this line, Calvin believed that one of the uses of the Mosaic Law was to reveal mankind's sinfulness and depravity. He believed that justification before God could only come from divine intervention in regeneration. He wrote, "The Mosaic Law would terrify the wicked and make the believer realize how dependent upon God one really is."

Discerning another use of the Law, Calvin saw it as a restrainer of the criminal element among unbelievers:

The second office of the law is to cause those who, unless constrained, feel no concern for justice and rectitude, when they hear its terrible sanctions, to be at least restrained by a fear of its penalties. And they are restrained...because, being chained as it were, they refrain from external acts, and repress their depravity within them, which otherwise would have wantonly discharged.

Church historian Philip Schaff comments: "Calvin's plea for the right and duty of the Christian magistrate to punish heresy by death, stands or falls with his theocratic theory and the binding authority of the Mosaic code. His arguments are chiefly drawn from the Jewish laws against idolatry and blasphemy, and from the examples of the pious kings of Israel" (n.d.).

Calvin imported Moses into the Grace Dispensation. He wrote that the Law "finds its place among believers in whose hearts the Spirit of God already lives and reigns...To this flesh the law serves as a whip, urging it, like a dull and tardy animal, forwards to its work; and even to the spiritual man, who is not yet delivered from the burden of the flesh, it will be a perpetual spur that will not permit him to loiter (Calvin, 1599, 1:323).

In contrast to this view, we would point to John 1:17: "For the Law was given through Moses; grace and truth were realized through Jesus Christ," and we would point to Luther's belief that the law does not prompt good works within the believer—that is the role of the Spirit of God.

In summarizing Calvin's theology, historian Will Durant, writing about Calvin's ideas of predestination to heaven and hell said, "We shall always find it hard to love the man who darkened the human soul with the most absurd and blasphemous conception of God in all the long and honored history of nonsense" (Durant, 1957, p. 490).

Ah, Those Puritans

The Puritans leave a bad taste in the mouths of historians. The taste was so bad that a word was born: puritanical. The word comes close to "tyrannical," and means "excessively strict in religious matters."

The fundamental reason for the rancid taste to the academic palate is because the Puritans made the mistake of identifying themselves with ancient Israel and made it their mission to impose the Law of God on their society. To add to their abrasiveness, they had a spiritual superiority complex which, when combined with the imposition of the Mosaic Law, led them to the Salem witchcraft trials.

When the Puritans arrived in the New World from England, they had a pretty exalted view of themselves: They were going to provide an example for the nations to follow so that this would lead directly to the Kingdom of God on Earth. Specifically, they wanted the England of their birth to see the New England they were going to establish in the New World, a New England of righteousness. Then, adopting this New England as their example, the Old England would repent and when that was done, the Old England would lead the nations of the world into the Kingdom of God. That is one high and lifted-up view of themselves!

Dr. Norman Geisler (1985) writes: "The Puritans persecuted those who would not conform. Many states required belief in God (theism) as a prerequisite for public office which lingered on the law books into the 1940s. This is consistent with the postmillennial need to establish God's rule on Earth." The superiority complex inherent in Puritanism showed itself clearly in the mid-1600s. "Some even argued that Jews ought to be readmitted to England, so that they would meet some of the godliest people on earth (Puritans), be converted, and thus hasten the beginning of the latter-day glory or millennium" (Gundry, 1977).

More evidence of the Puritans' self-appointed superiority was their conviction that they were the chosen people whom God had elected to build "Jerusalem" in England. John Winthrop, in "A Modell of Christian Charity" (1630), expressed the belief that the Puritans were the chosen people of God.

In 1630, when Winthrop spoke to Puritan colonists sailing to the New World on the ship *Arbella*, he referred to God as "Our God" and to the Puritans as "his oune [own] people." He reminded his fellow colonists: "We are entered into Covenant with Him. . . . wee [we] shall be as a city upon a hill. The eies [eyes] of all people are upon us." Winthrop believed that the Puritans had a duty to fulfill their covenant with God by serving as an example of an ideal Christian community to the world. In return, God would protect his chosen people (cited in Gleason, n.d.).

As time went on, the Puritans became more and more adamant that Moses and his Law were the model, and consequently, they incorporated its penalties; after all,

The mission of the church is to make disciples.

a law isn't a law unless its breakage brings penalties. Therefore, the Puritans enacted capital punishment for heretics, adulterers, and blasphemers. This is one reason that people react so strongly when they hear of Christians trying to "take over the government"—and rightly so, if their intent is to impose the Mosaic Law on America. (The mission of the church is not to take over the government; the mission of the church is to make disciples.)

Excursus: Dissenters in Paradise

There were dissenters in the Puritans' colony: Roger Williams opposed the idea that Israel's Law ought to be the model for New England's civil and religious life or anywhere else and therefore clashed with the Puritans on that basic tenet. He also collided with the Puritan laws, especially the one requiring church attendance, saying that true faith was a matter of personal commitment and could not be compelled. "Forced faith stinks in God's nostrils," he told his congregation.

Anne Hutchinson was a member of the Massachusetts Bay Colony. She spoke of a spirit-centered theology which held that God's grace could be directly bestowed through faith. She was a free grace believer who said that God's promise of salvation did not depend on a minister, a church, or a worship service. She accused some of the ministers of teaching salvation by works. This went against the Puritan ministers' orthodox view, which dictated that people must live according to the Bible's precepts and perform good deeds.

The magistrates put Hutchinson on trial, excommunicated her from the church, and banished the expecting mother from the colony. In April 1638, she and her children, along with a few others, began a six-day journey in the snow to Rhode Island, a more tolerant colony with more religious freedom. The next month, she went into labor, but her baby died. After her husband died, she moved to New Amsterdam. In 1643, she and five of her children were killed in an Indian raid. In a galling statement born of that Puritan high-and-mighty superiority, John Winthrop said that he viewed her violent death as a sign of God's final judgment on her blasphemy.

In 1922, a statue of Hutchinson was erected on the grounds of the Massachusetts State House. In 1945, the legislature voted to revoke her banishment.

Puritan Postmillennialism

The Puritans believed that the church would enjoy a time of prosperity and purity of doctrine, worship, and practice. They saw the church as moving ever onward and upward in triumph toward the ultimate establishment of God's Kingdom on Earth. They believed that the governments of the nations would recognize that their primary purpose was the cause of the church. This would usher in the millennium, and, at the end of God's Kingdom on Earth, Christ would return to be seen by all and to execute judgment on all who had opposed Him.

Gundry (1977, p. 48) writes about the pervasiveness of the Puritan postmillennialism in America:

> The Puritans brought the doctrine to New England. Some even considered the Indians of the Americas to be descendants of the ten lost tribes of Israel. Thus their conversion to Christianity would have special significance for the bringing in of the millennial age. Through this Puritan influence, varieties of postmillennialism were the dominant eschatology in American theology until at least the last quarter of the nineteenth century. Jonathan Edwards gave special place and development to that doctrine. In 1742 he conjectured that the Great Awakening, especially in New England, might "prove the dawn of that glorious day." Charles Finney, almost one hundred years later, lamented that if Christians in the United States had gone to work ten years earlier, "the millennium would have fully come in the United States before this day."

The Puritans didn't comprehend that the church is never called "Israel" in the New Testament. The two are always kept separate, even in the oft-cited Galatians 6:16 text, in which Paul is speaking of Jews in the Galatian churches. Had the Puritans been dispensational in their theology, they would never have thought that Old England, New England, or any other gentile nation was God's elect nation which would lead other countries into the establishment of the Kingdom of God on Earth. What they did was read Israel into the church, a

The church is never called "Israel" in the New Testament.

classic case of eisegesis: that is, reading one's theology *into* the Bible rather than drawing one's theology *from* the Bible.

Both the Scriptures and experience never present evidence of the church triumphant. The parables of Matthew 13 predict the progression of the church in the Grace Dispensation to be downward, leavened, and corrupted. The extended string of parables in Matthew 13 predicts Satan's planting tares (unbelievers) among the wheat (believers). So

> **Both the Scriptures and experience never present evidence of the church triumphant.**

prolific is this satanic sowing that the tares must be harvested in bundles. Yet, this gathering the tares into bundles is not for now, but for when Christ returns. It is useless for the church to engage in reform movements such as reforms to eliminate drunkenness, restrain immorality, and purge politics of its inherent corruption.

> **It is useless for the church to engage in reform movements**

Billy Sunday, the foremost evangelist of the early 20th century, wasted his time, squandered his resources, and devalued his ministry with his incessant crusades for prohibition in America. He should have recognized it as being against the command of Christ for believers as given in the Great Commission. *The mission of the church is to go into the world and make disciples*, first by sowing the seed of the gospel, then leading the new believers in following Christ. The mission of the church is not as the Puritans believed, because they confused Israel with the church. It is not for Christians or the church to take over the government or to try to reform the government. The Christian is all for good government, but not for the taking over of government.

The course of this age, according to the Parable of the Leaven, is a growing and inward corruption of the Christian message. Into the substantial meal of true doctrine, Satan introduces the leaven,

In Scripture, leaven is always the symbol of evil.

making the food of God's people less substantive and, therefore, tastier to the world. In Scripture, leaven is always the symbol of evil. Christ predicts in the Parable of the Leaven that a foreign substance will invade the church and will spread throughout the whole meal of pure doctrine.

In the Parable of the Mustard Seed, fowls come and nest in the herb — an herb grown into the monstrosity of a tree. When the world accepts the church, the spirituality of the church is snowballing down a steep cliff. 2 Timothy 3:13 warns: "But evil men and impostors will proceed

When the world accepts the church, the spirituality of the church is snowballing down a steep cliff.

from bad to worse, deceiving and being deceived."

Over and over again, the New Testament authors warn against and predict apostasy in the church: "But the Spirit explicitly says that in later times some will fall away from the faith, paying attention to deceitful spirits and doctrines of demons ..." (1 Timothy 4:1). Paul specifically warns of wolves arising from within the church, arising from the elders themselves: "Be on guard for yourselves and for all the flock, among which the Holy Spirit has made you overseers, to shepherd the church of God which He purchased with His own blood. I know that after my departure savage wolves will come in among you, not sparing the flock" (Acts 20:28–29).

Experience shows the fallacy of the idea of the church triumphant. Islam, not Christianity, is almost to the point of being the religion of the majority of the earth's population. After all this time, we do not see an increasingly triumphant church.

Even in the so-called "Bible Belt," we find churchgoers—yes, even long-time church members who have attended their churches from the nursery into adulthood—to be infected with works for salvation, confused even to the point of having no idea of the

> **The church triumphant does not exist.**

definition of *grace*, trying to live a good life, trying to keep the Ten Commandments, even rejecting outright and with extreme prejudice anything about faith alone in Christ alone. The church triumphant does not exist.

Christ described the church not as a conquering physical and political force, but as those who would struggle, being pilgrims rather than being at home on this planet, hated and persecuted for His name's sake. In His Upper Room Discourse, Jesus, preparing the disciples for the Church Age, told them: "If the world hates you, you know that it has hated Me before *it* hated you. If you were of the world, the world would love its own; but because you are not of the world, but I chose you out of the world, because of this the world hates you" (John 15:18–19). He continued, "These things I have spoken to you, so that in Me you may have peace. In the world you have tribulation, but take courage; I have overcome the world" (John 16:33).

Evangelist D. L. Moody, the foremost American evangelist of the 19th century, said it well (1877):

> I look on this world as a wrecked vessel. God has given me a life-boat, and said to me, "Moody, save all you can." God will come in judgment and burn up this world, but the children of God don't belong to this world; they are in it but not of it, like a ship in the water. This world is getting darker, and its ruin is coming nearer and nearer. If you have any friends of this wreck unsaved, you had better lose no time in getting them off.

8

So What?

We've come a long way since page one. If you're convinced by the main theses of this book — i.e., that the Law was for Israel alone, the church is not Israel, and the believer is to repudiate (lay down) the Law as a way of life — then you're most likely asking, "What do I do now?" That's the subject of this chapter, which will conclude our reasoning through the Scriptures.

False doctrine has always been on the scene to oppose true doctrine. There never has been a shortage of false teachers, going back to the legalists whom Paul, Peter, and James opposed in Acts 15, to Marcion the Heretic, and Cerinthus who propagated what Paul called "doctrines of demons" (1 Timothy 4:1). The New Testament authors filled their letters with warnings to alert the churches that false teachers were abroad in the land (2 Corinthians 11:3–4; Galatians 1:6, 7, 9; 1 Timothy 1:19–20; Hebrews 13:9; 2 Peter 2:1; 1 John 4:1; Titus 1:10 14; Jude 4; etc.). Paul forewarned the elders of the church at Ephesus that savage wolves would arise from within their number, false teachers who would draw away many (not a few) from the faith (Acts 20:28–30).

False doctrine has always been on the scene to oppose true doctrine.

Jesus had earlier warned of such teachers, calling them "wolves" who appear to be sheep (Matthew 7:15). He also warned of false teachers to come (Matthew 24:5). In John 10, He expounded on this at length, contrasting the false shepherds with the Good Shepherd. As He went into detail about false shepherds in Israel,

He called them "hired hands," using a Greek word for fishermen who worked for pay.

By the sheer volume of such alerts, the reader of the New Testament can see that the Bible is serious about the impact of false teachers and their teaching. We aren't to dismiss such words of warning to the wise nor take them casually. Both the lost and the sheep are in danger when false teachers twist the gospel into works and deny or tamper with the foundations of the faith.

False Teaching, Specifically

Dr. S. Lewis Johnson (2006) writes:

> One of the most serious problems facing the orthodox Christian church today is the problem of legalism. One of the most serious problems facing the church in Paul's day was the problem of legalism. In every day it is the same. Legalism wrenches the joy of the Lord from the Christian believer, and with the joy of the Lord goes his power for vital worship and vibrant service. Nothing is left but cramped, somber, dull and listless profession. The truth is betrayed, and the glorious name of the Lord becomes a synonym for a gloomy kill-joy. The Christian under law is a miserable parody of the real thing.

James S. Stewart (1935) enumerates the three marks of legalism:

> It is essentially "a religion of *redemption through human effort*," a method by which man may build his own highway to the heavens. In this it is a direct contradiction of the truth of Ephesians 2:8–10. In the second place, there is "its *tendency to import a mercenary spirit into religion*." A man, pointing to his achievements, becomes able to demand of God the reward of eternal life. And, furthermore, by multiplying regulations and requirements, he is able to continue increasing

his claim upon God. In this it is a direct contradiction of 1 Corinthians 4:2–7. Finally, legalism has a "*fondness for negatives.*" We are reminded of the "thou shalt nots" of the Ten Commandments and of the modern taboos invented by contemporary churchmen. In this, legalism is a contradiction of the truth of Colossians 2:20–23.

Legalism is not legalism because it recognizes standards; legalism is legalism because it says that one may conform to such standards by one's own efforts and can gain merit and a right standing before God by such accomplishments.

Legalism is as ancient as the fall of man; it began with Adam, his needle, thread, and fig leaves. Fallen man has always had a love affair with legalism because it always brings the flesh an opportunity to look good. Legalism is the breeding ground for peacocks in the church.

When the believer is obsessed with legalistic practices, he is out of touch with the Head of the body, the Lord Jesus. Physically, when a part of the body is out of touch with the head, paralysis results. Just so, when legalism leavens its way through a church, it paralyzes the growth of the believer in grace and places him in an ecclesiastical iron lung.

Jesus said: "Abide in me, and I in you. As the branch cannot bear fruit of itself, except it abide in the vine; *no more can ye, except you abide in me.* I am the vine, you are the branches: he that abides in me, and I in him, the same brings forth much fruit: *for without me you can do nothing*"

Legalism disconnects the believer from a fruit-producing life.

(John 15:4–5). Legalism disconnects the believer from a fruit-producing life. Legalism blocks believers from the abundant life they could have enjoyed.

179

Steven J. Cole (2013) observes,

> It is noteworthy how He deliberately did things to provoke the legalists. He could have healed people on any other day of the week, but He often did it on the Sabbath. He could have been more discreet in violating the Pharisees' rules, but He did it openly. When a Pharisee invited Jesus to dinner, He could have gone along with their elaborate hand-washing custom, but He deliberately ignored it. When they questioned Him about it, He could have been more polite, but He blasted them for their hypocrisy. When a lawyer pointed out that Jesus had offended them as well, He didn't say, "I'm sorry! I didn't mean to offend you good folks." He said, "Woe to you lawyers as well!" Jesus confronted legalism as sin.

Jesus could have shared a dinner with priests and Sadducees, but instead he ate with a man who spent his adult life ruining other people's lives and betraying his Jewish heritage *(cf.* Luke 19:1–10).

How Do I Know If I'm in a System of Legalism: Tithing

Does your church demand 10% of your income? Listen to "The Baptist Standard" of January 10, 2013:

> The principal topic of discussion at the morning session of the Southern Baptist Convention was the report of the committee on tithing.... The committee recommended the adoption of the tithing system, and that several state conventions, district associations, the pastors, churches and missionary societies educate the people up to paying systematically to God not less than one-tenth of their income" (as reported in *The New York Times*, May 12, 1895).

From its beginning in 1845, the Southern Baptist Convention has emphasized giving. Still today, the SBC is among denominations that encourage believers to give at least 10% of their income to their local church. Leaders of the two major faith-based financial service ministries—Crown Financial Ministries and Dave Ramsey's Financial Peace University—do as well.

> Those who promote the 10% concept usually cite Malachi 3:8–11, especially verse 10, which emphasizes bringing the "full tenth into the storehouse" (*Holman Christian Standard Bible*, 2009). The passage promises that God will "open the floodgates of heaven and pour out a blessing for you without measure."

Malachi 3 is the golden text which legalism has tarnished trying to convince believers in the Grace Dispensation to go back under the Law, so let's examine it:

> Will a man rob God? Yet you are robbing Me! But you say, 'How have we robbed You?' In tithes and offerings. You are cursed with a curse, for you are robbing Me, the whole nation of you! Bring the whole tithe into the storehouse, so that there may be food in My house, and test Me now in this," says the LORD of hosts, "if I will not open for you the windows of heaven and pour out for you a blessing until it overflows. Then I will rebuke the devourer for you, so that it will not destroy the fruits of the ground; nor will your vine in the field cast its grapes," says the LORD of hosts.

The first question to ask is, "To whom is Malachi speaking?" We see that he's speaking to "the whole nation." So, the question is, "What nation is the prophet denouncing?" We go back to Malachi 1:1 to find the answer: "The oracle of the word of the LORD *to Israel* through Malachi." So, we see that God is denouncing the nation of Israel. (It's impossible for Malachi to be speaking to the church because the Bible never calls the church "a nation." (Peter addresses his readers as "the holy nation," but Peter is writing to "the diaspora." *Diaspora* is a technical term in the New Testament, referring only to Jews. The Jews he was addressing were those scattered in the various regions of Turkey who were believers in Christ. Peter is not writing to a church. These converted Jews are the true "holy nation," the remnant.)

The church has no national homeland; in fact, the church did not come into existence until Acts 2. Even in Christ's day, He Himself referred to the church as something to come, not something which "was" or "is:" He announced, "I also say to you that you are Peter, and upon this rock *I will* build My church; and the gates of Hades will not overpower it" (Matthew 16:18).

The second question to ask is, "What's the storehouse?" The storehouse was God's house, the Temple. "There were special rooms in the temple devoted to storing the gifts the Israelites brought" (*cf.* 1 Kings 7:51; Nehemiah 10:38, 13:12) (Constable, n.d.). The church has no physical temple; the Temple was the central sanctuary of Israel.

The third question to ask is, "What are the tithes?" There were several kinds of tithes: (1) the tenth of the remainder after the first-fruits were taken, this amount going to Levites for their livelihood (Leviticus 27:30–33); (2) the tenth paid by Levites to the priests (Numbers 18:26–28); (3) the second tenth paid by the congregation for the needs of the Levites and their own families at the tabernacle (Deuteronomy 12:18); and (4) another tithe every third year for the poor (Deuteronomy 14:28, 29) (Feinberg, 1951).

The fourth question to ask is, "In what dispensation is God addressing Israel?" Of course, He is speaking only to the nation Israel during the Dispensation of the Law. Therefore, these instructions are for Israel while the Law reigned over them.

What About Melchizedek?
What about Genesis, a book that describes events before the laying-down of the Law at Mount Sinai? In Genesis 14, also referred to

in Hebrews 7, Abraham meets a gentile believer and gives him a tenth of all the spoils. Legalists use this text to instruct church members to tithe. But we would note that Genesis 14 and Hebrews 7 are *descriptions* of events, not *prescriptions* based on an event; there is no command to the church to tithe in these descriptions. (Bible students must always ask themselves, "Am I reading a description, that is, a relating of events, or am I reading a prescription, that is, a command?" This would save much confusion.)

What About Jesus' Conversation with the Pharisees?

It's ironic that legalists seek to legitimize their insistence on tithing by Jesus' strongest condemnation of legalism. During a dialogue with the Pharisees, Jesus said, "Woe to you, scribes and Pharisees, hypocrites! For you tithe mint and dill and cumin, and have neglected the weightier provisions of the law: justice and mercy and faithfulness; but these are the things you should have done without neglecting the others" (Matthew 23: 23). Legalists pounce on the words, "but these are the things you should have done without neglecting the others." In other words, Jesus is saying, "You should have tithed." Is that what He's saying? Of course it is, but the question is, once again, "To whom is He speaking and when did He say this?"

> *It's ironic that legalists seek to legitimize their insistence on tithing by Jesus' strongest condemnation of legalism.*

He's speaking to Jews living under the Dispensation of the Law, and Israelites living in that dispensation were commanded to tithe. *Jesus is not speaking to the church.*

Grace Giving
Paul outlines grace giving in 1 Cor. 16 and 2 Cor. 8–9. Dr. Constable (n.d.) summarizes the New Testament method of giving: However, the New Covenant under which Christians live

never specified the amount or that we should give back to God of what He has given to us. Rather it teaches that we should give regularly, sacrificially, as the Lord has prospered us, and joyfully (cf. 1 Cor. 16:2; 2 Cor. 8:1–4, 9–14; 2 Cor. 9:2, 7, 12; Phil. 4:10–19). In harmony with the principle of grace that marks the present dispensation, the Lord leaves the amount we give back to Him unspecified and up to us. Christians who sit under a steady diet of preaching that majors on God's grace often give far more than 10 percent (Constable, n.d.).

How Do I Know If I'm Under a System of Legalism: Rules

We all have rules, codes of conduct, by which we live. There's a maxim, "A man's home is his castle." It's a saying based on English law which speaks to the sanctity of one's property and the right to protect it from intruders who would do harm to the homeowner. But it also came to signify that a man is sovereign in his own home; that is, he may do what he pleases within the law.

Christian homes may have various rules of conduct that violate the Bill of Rights. For example, in the home in which I grew up, we had two rules of grammar: no one was ever to say "ain't" and no one was ever to end a sentence with the preposition "at," as in, "Where's he at?" Four-letter words were also forbidden. So, there was no freedom of speech in our castle.

There was no freedom of the press either: no one was to have a subscription to "The Daily Worker," a publication of the Communist Party USA.

Now, those rules didn't make us legalists, because nobody thought that by keeping those rules, we would gain a right standing before God. Legalism rears its serpentine head when we believe that, by keeping our rules or God's commands, we gain a favorable standing or thereby improve our standing with

Him. Legalism reigns when we believe that we are superior to others and when we complicate matters by trying to impose those rules on others. Paul speaks to the point in Colossians 2:16–17: "Therefore no one is to act as your judge in regard to food or drink or in respect to a festival or a new moon or a Sabbath day— things which are a mere shadow of what is to come; but the substance belongs to Christ."

> *Legalism reigns when we believe that we are superior to others.*

Legalists are like politicians: they want to control your life. In Colossae, the false teachers were putting the yoke of the Law on the believers regarding the five things Paul lists (including restricting their diets and making them observe certain days), all of which were aspects of Judaism. Paul calls these "shadows." Shadows are dispersed by the light and the light of grace has come.

Warren Wiersbe (1981) wisely points out:

> Sad to say, there are many Christians who actually believe that some person, religious system, or discipline can add something to their spiritual experience. But they already have everything they ever will need in the person and work of Jesus Christ... The believing Gentiles in Colossae never were under the Law of Moses since that Law was given only to Israel (Rom. 9:4). It seems strange that, now that they were Christians, they would want to submit themselves to Jewish legalism!

That First Drink

Each believer has his own code of conduct apart from the Bible. One of the rules that I've had all of my life is that I do not drink alcohol. Not once; never ever. I promised my parents that I never would do such a thing. However, I can't find my rule anywhere in the

Bible. There is a prohibition against drunkenness, but not against drinking. This rule, therefore, is my rule for myself. In no way do I think that I've gained some of Christ's righteousness credited to my account by keeping this rule, nor do I try to impose it on others, nor do I think that I'm more spiritual than those who imbibe.

I have my reasons for the rule, one of which is that one out of every ten people who take their first drink become alcoholics. So, I reason, "Would I get on a plane if I knew that one out of every ten crash?" My answer is, "No, I would not." But that's my rule for me and me alone. My reasons, in my opinion, are good reasons, and I may point them out to others, but in no way do I shun those who disagree with me, nor do I think them to be inferior to me.

Those Cosmetics

It's interesting that "Christian" rules vary depending on the section of the country. A Christian woman in Yankee Land may have a rule that forbids the wearing of makeup, while the Christian woman in the South paints the barn. This rule, like my no-drink rule, is not a biblical rule. (The Bible does tell the Christian wife not to use her outward appearance to manipulate her unsaved husband.)

The Yankee Christian may go the noncosmetic route, while her Southern belle of a sister in Christ may apply the lipstick. Both are within their rights to make their choices, if they do so "as unto the Lord, being persuaded in their own mind." Each has the freedom to exercise that choice without being judged, condemned, ostracized, or excommunicated by the other.

Each has the freedom to exercise that choice without being judged, condemned, ostracized, or excommunicated by the other.

Tripping the Light Fantastic

In some Christian circles, dancing is taboo. The intent of this rule is to set up a barrier, which, if crossed, might lead to other activities which are sinful. So, they reason, "Let's put up a barrier to keep our youth from getting into sin." The problem is that the barrier they build isn't sin in and of itself, so they've called something sin which is not sin.

For some people, dancing may lead to an impure mental attitude or activity, so if they choose not to dance on that basis, that's all well and good. But other believers see dancing as a wholesome activity, even a healthy exercise, and for them it doesn't lead to other things. So be it. Let each believer choose to dance or not to dance.

Those are our own rules and we're not to be considered legalists for having such rules—as long as we don't think they earn us any right relationship or Brownie points with God. But let's go back to recognizing a legalistic church.

Sundays: No Fun in the Sun

You know you're in a system of legalism if your church lays down rules for you to keep on Sunday as if it were that aberration called "the Christian Sabbath." The church in which I grew up instructed us not to work on Sundays and not to buy anything on Sundays, and the church gave us bumper stickers to that effect so we could tell others what to do and show them what good Christians we were (that is, a lot better than they). We were expected to fold up like a tent on Sundays; for kids, Sunday became Nofunday. (Fortunately, my parents didn't follow the church on that one. I had a lot of fun on Sundays, with no guilt.) The problem is that churches take the rules God gave to Israel for Saturday and transfer them to Sunday and kids grow up hating Christianity.

Morphing Rules

"Shape-shifting" is a tradition that exists in most native cultures. It's the supposed metamorphosis of a person into an animal or other form. Another type of shape-shifting occurs in legalistic churches. No, the congregants don't turn into foxes, but you know you're in a system of legalism when their manmade rules shape-shift into rules straight from the Bible, as if those rules were God-ordained and clearly stated in the Bible, chapter and verse.

Watch Out!
You are in a system of legalism if others condemn, ostracize, or excommunicate you if you don't observe their manufactured rules. For example, one church states that if a person drives a beer truck, that person is not eligible for membership. If a member of the church is discovered to be driving such a vehicle and therefore delivering said contraband, it's as if he had a personal connection with Al Capone, and the offending member must resign his membership immediately. If he does not, he will face excommunication: that is, the church will strip away his membership for him.

> *You are in a system of legalism if others condemn, ostracize, or excommunicate you if you don't observe their manufactured rules.*

Lights Out!
Unfortunately, some of the most egregious legalism infects Christian schools. Rules proliferate, penalties abound, and students are both encouraged and rewarded for reporting each other if rules are broken or slightly bent. Many schools have a provision for self-confession upon breakage: one student confessed her sin of using a flashlight to study under a blanket after the rule said, "Lights out." Punishment was administered. She was 22 years old, yet was deemed not to have enough sense to go to sleep until told to do so!

Rules breed more rules, as schools prescribe the students' study time and where they may sit in the library (to ensure that they're with their own gender). The rules designate the stairways they may use: one for the males, another for the females. Rules monitor their music, a ruler measures their hair. Suddenly a student finds his computer confiscated and under examination because another student has reported him to the authorities. Even his off-campus behavior is regulated and monitored. He is under a type of surveillance in which the school is like something out of **1984**. If there's not a rule for everything, the school will invent one. It's a never-ending process. The father of a student at a Christian college summed it up nicely: "The school treats its students as if they were 12 years old."

The New Testament is devoid of a detailed list of rules. It's nothing like the writings of the rabbis, which contained invented rule after invented rule or "The Didache" (Lightfoot, n.d.), a discipleship manual for the church written after the age of the apostles and before 300 AD. "The Didache" ("The Teaching") listed rules concerning a proper baptism:

> *The New Testament is devoid of a detailed list of rules.*

> This is how you should baptize ... baptize in the name of the Father and the Son and the Holy Spirit, in running water. If you do not have running water, then baptize in still water. The water should be cold, but if you do not have cold water, then use warm. If you have neither, then just pour water on the head three times in the name of the Father, the Son and the Holy Spirit. Both the one who is baptized and the one who baptizes should fast beforehand, along with any others who are able, the one that is baptized being told to fast for a day or two.

Speaking of fasting, the manual prescribed, apparently without seeing its own hypocrisy, that, "Your fasting should not be like the hypocrites'. They fast on Monday and Thursday: you should fast on Wednesday and Friday." This is a classic example of the need to cast the beam out of one's own eye before removing a pollutant from another's.

The New Testament is principle-oriented, not list-oriented. Colossians 3:17 is an example of this principled orientation: "Whatever you do in word or deed, do all in the name of the Lord Jesus, giving thanks through Him to God the Father." This principle may be applied to all situations that arise in life: whatever you do, think, or plan, do so in harmony with the revelation of the character of the Lord Jesus. It means asking, "Is this appropriate for someone who is identified with Christ?" This is very much different from the Law-oriented way of life with its specific commands, lists, and penalties for every situation.

Get Serious

There's a story from church history about the Apostle John that was recorded in the second-century book *Against Heresies* by Irenaeus. Irenaeus had been a disciple of Polycarp, who had been a disciple of John. It's from this direct line to John that Irenaeus got his information.

At the end of the first century, there was a Gnostic heretic named Cerinthus. Among other things, he denied the Virgin Birth, denied that Jesus was the Christ His entire life, and taught that Christians were required to follow the Mosaic Law.

One day, John went inside a public bathhouse, but quickly spotted Cerinthus inside. John immediately ran out of the building, exclaiming to those with him, "Let us fly, lest even the bathhouse fall down, because Cerinthus, the enemy of the truth, is within!" (Against Heresies, 3.3.4).

That's serious!

The believer must have the attitude that legalism—the false teaching that God accepts one based on one's works (being baptized, persevering to the end, denying self, taking up one's cross, following Christ, obeying Christ, making Christ the Lord of one's life, forsaking one's sins, keeping the Golden Rule, observing the Ten Commandments, etc.) — is so serious that the believer must deploy one of various options stated in the Word of God. There's a problem with these options, a problem because we're human beings: it takes a strong and spiritually healthy believer to put them into action. A weak, sickly believer doesn't have the vitality to do so.

The First Option

Paul gives the first option when believers, such as the Christians in the Galatian churches, find themselves in a situation infected by the virus of legalism. Paul gives the solution by using typology from the Old Testament.

Abraham and Sarah had a lapse of faith, and, in their impatience, instead of waiting on God for the son He promised would come from them, they adopted a worldly plan which was customary, perfectly legal, and totally acceptable at the time. They decided to produce the heir by surrogate: their servant Hagar would bear a son from Abraham. The plan worked (in their opinion) and Ishmael was born. But the problem was that he wasn't the God-ordained heir to whom the Abrahamic Covenant would be given; this proxy plan wasn't God's agenda. (Even though a child was born, which some would say was an indication of God's will for Abraham, circumstances are not an indication of God's plan; God's Word is.) He had previously revealed His will: the heir would come via a miracle — by the rejuvenation of the ever-aging Abraham and Sarah.

Their proxy plan brought nothing but tension into the family tent. There's tension and then there's *tension*, but there's no tension like family tension. The anxiety began even before the birth of Ishmael; there was hatred between the two women and then came a rupture between Abraham and Sarah. Two women in one family hating each other (one jealous, the other gloating) doesn't make for a joyful home or wedded bliss.

Not only was there that tension, but there was also new tension when the heir, Isaac, did come in God's way and in God's time (Abraham was 100 years old when Isaac was born). Ishmael began to mock Isaac when the younger boy was weaned; young Isaac's life was in danger and this was noticed, not by his father, but, as is usually the case, by his mother, Sarah. Sarah notified Abraham of the danger to their child and bluntly advised, "Throw the woman and her son out!" God told Abraham to follow Sarah's advice. He did, but the fruit of that proxy plan still brought unimaginable misery to the descendants of Abraham, Isaac, and Jacob for generation after generation down to the present day.

Paul uses the typology of the events and people to advise the churches in Galatia that were under the hammer and tongs of the legalists. The bond servant Hagar represents Mount Sinai (a place far from the Promised Land), the Covenant of works (the Mosaic Law), and the earthly Jerusalem under the control of the legalists in Paul's day.

Sarah represents the heavenly Mount Zion, the Jerusalem which is above, the Abrahamic Covenant, and grace.

In Paul's analogy, we see that the legalist will always persecute the person of grace. The situation is never reversed; legalism always persecutes grace, grace never persecutes legalism.

> **The legalist will always persecute the person of grace.**

Why is this? Why does the legalist always torment the person of grace? It's because the grace believer disturbs the legalist, because grace clearly points out that the things the legalist does don't have any merit before God. Grace declares that the legalist's trust has not met the right object: Christ. Grace delivers the message that the object of the legalist's faith is misplaced, as it lies in his works as the means by which he thinks he can earn or bribe his way into a right standing with God.

So, when the grace person says, "No, you're not justified by the things you do, but only by the cross of Jesus Christ," this stirs up the legalist to rebel and reject the idea. The hubris of the legalists has been wounded and, like wounded animals, they strike back. The tormenting begins. This has occurred again and again in church history.

What kind of a life is it when one is afraid to be seen doing anything? This acquiescence to the legalists is the opposite of what the Lord Jesus did and of Paul tells the Galatians to do, as we will see. It is the opposite of how Paul dealt with Peter in Galatians 2.

Legalists remind me of the opening scene of *Mutiny on the Bounty* (1935). (I saw it on TV, years and years later.) Clark Gable is leading a press gang for the British Royal Navy. Press gangs consisted of 10 to 12 men, led by an officer, who would roam the streets looking for likely "volunteers," whom they would take into custody and force (press) into naval service against their will. Press gangs were violent in their methods of recruitment. They existed because recruiting sailors voluntarily was difficult; the conditions on board ships were harsh, and serving in the navy, especially in wartime, was dangerous.

This is the way legalists are, pressing others into the service of their rules through sermons, shaming, and threats. In such a situation, the leadership is "lording it over them," an attitude and action definitely forbidden by 1 Peter 5:3.

Other members of the press gang of legalists are authors, many of whom are well-known in diverse Christian circles, as the following quotes gathered by Roy Aldrich (1961) attest:

- "The law is a rule of life for believers, reminding them of their duties and leading them in the way of life and salvation." Louis Berkhof (graduate of and teacher at Calvin Theological Seminary, Grand Rapids)

- "The moral precepts are not repealed. The entire decalogue is brought into the Christian code by a distinct injunction of its separate parts." Richard Watson (Methodist)

- "Grace has in no sense superseded law. Obedience to law puts one in the midstream of God's purpose." P. B. Fitzwater (Dean of the Bible Department, Manchester College; Professor at Moody Bible Institute)

- "Christ does not free us from the law as a rule of life." Augustus Strong (Baptist, Calvinist, and one never known to laugh out loud in public)

- "Christians should recite the commandments (as their creeds) to keep in memory what they must do to enter into life." William B. Pope (Methodist)

- "The law is a declaration of the will of God for man's salvation." Oswald T. Allis (Presbyterian)

- "Genuine sanctification will show itself in habitual respect to God's law, and habitual effort to live in obedience to it as the rule of life. There is no greater mistake than to suppose that a Christian has nothing to do with the law and the Ten Commandments, because he cannot be justified by keeping them." J. C. Ryle (Anglican)

- "If, therefore, it is heresy for a Christian to boast that he is experimentally 'dead indeed unto sin,' it must be no less a heresy to boast that one is actually 'not under law' as a rule of conduct for his life. For what is sin if it be not the transgression of law." L. E. Maxwell (president of Prairie Bible Institute)

- "The liberty we enjoy as Christians is not a licentious liberty: Though Christ has redeemed us from the curse of the law he has not freed us from the obligation of it." Matthew Henry (Presbyterian)

Unfortunately, we also see another fact of life in churches today: In such a situation, the grace believer always bows to the legalist. Ron Phillips, looking back on his younger days as a rural pastor in 1956, tells this story:

[My] first assignment was leading a congregation in rural Alabama and, in those days going to movies — even biblical ones — was frowned upon in the Baptist community. When I and my wife wanted to see "The Ten Commandments" [or any film] we drove to Montgomery or Birmingham to evade prying eyes and wagging tongues. ... We didn't want to do anything around our little town because we didn't want anyone to see us. We didn't think it was wrong, but it wasn't acceptable back then.

Phillips admits the power of a legalistic culture when he says, "We didn't want to do *anything* around our little town because we didn't want anyone to see us." Yet, as we've seen, Jesus played the part of a provocateur when it came to offending the rigid and judgmental legalists; He deliberately broke their rules with high visibility, even announcing that He was going to do so before He did it (Luke 19:1–10).

The Galatian Analogy

In Paul's analogy, we see that the persecutor (Ishmael) was close to the persecuted (Isaac). They lived together, ate together, and engaged in daily activities together. This could not continue, and Sarah recognized it and proposed the solution.

The Abraham-Sarah-Hagar-Ishmael-Isaac situation was like expecting the Sharia law of Islam to coexist with the American Constitution. It's impossible because they are fundamentally incompatible. Sharia law has no Bill of Rights. Under Sharia law, there is no freedom of speech, no freedom of the press, no freedom of worship.

There is no way to establish a live-and-let-live policy between the two. A society cannot remain a unified society trying to live under both systems. To try to reconcile the two would shred a nation, just as churches are torn apart by trying to accommodate legalism and grace for the sake of nickels and noses.

In such a tolerant law-and-grace tent, there will always be an uneasy truce along with unrelieved tension; no one can live a healthy and productive life in a situation of continual tension. Stress will be present during the 11:00 a.m. service from the prelude to the benediction. Committee meetings and business meetings will be conducted on tenterhooks. Tension will be the uninvited guest at every church social. Like an anchor, it will drag down every attempt at ministry. It will corrode every prayer meeting. The members may put on the face and play the game as if all is well, but they know better — all is not well and can never be.

Instead of acquiescing to the legalist, Paul says, "Separate" (Galatians 4:30). The reason for such a painful command is that works as a means of salvation and faith alone in Christ alone as the means of salvation can find no common ground. There can be no dialoguing to detente. Grace is non-negotiable.

Two Ways to Separate

In some situations, Paul commands the elders to take charge and shut the false teachers down by removing their platforms (Titus 1:10–11). This is obedience to the "Throw out the bond-woman with her son" command (Galatians 4:30). In the Titus text, Paul specifically singles out the legalists: "For there are many rebellious men, empty talkers and deceivers, *especially those of the circumcision*, who must be silenced because they are upsetting whole families, teaching things they should not teach for the sake of sordid gain." In this text, Paul singles out the legalists for the silencing, as he writes, "especially those of the circumcision."

Paul gave these instructions to the elders of the house churches on Crete. The elders are the ones God designates to shepherd the flock (Acts 20:28), and they are to do what shepherds do: protect the flock by repelling the wolves. Obeying this command requires elders in each church who are spiritually strong and healthy, those with the courage of Gideon's three hundred. Elders who put numbers first are not biblical elders.

> *The elders are the ones God designates to shepherd the flock... protect the flock by repelling the wolves.*

Paul's instruction is blunt: "throw out the legalists." Dr. Robert P. Lightner (1985) details what happens when the elders are disobedient to Paul's command:

> The longer an error is condoned or tolerated, the easier it is to compromise the truth. Somehow a conditioning process goes on. An unhealthy toleration of false doctrine usually leads to accommodation to it. When falsehood is left unchecked, unexposed, or unopposed, it gradually seems less and less objectionable. It looks more and more like merely a weak and watered-down form of truth, though, to be sure, a less desirable option than the truth.

Another Type of Separation

There are churches which have been so corrupted by legalism for so long (generations) that the leaven of the Pharisees has become the established orthodoxy of those churches... and woe be to any who challenge it! They will find themselves the victim of character assassination, plots, lies, secret meetings, open and vicious challenges, anonymous letters and mailings to the congregation. (Christ warned that the wolves are *fierce*.) The problem is that in such a church, the legalists *are* the entrenched elders, the dominating deacons, and the teachers, the direct descendants of Diotrephes (3 John 9).

Being realistic, the archangel Michael with a flaming sword couldn't change such an abhorrent situation. In such a case, healthy believers should remove themselves, their wallets, and their families from the premises. Knowing the seriousness of the sin of legalism, they will take their wallets with them and no longer support the church that has become an ecclesiastical press gang.

> *Healthy believers should remove themselves.*

To summarize, the two options for separation are: (1) throwing the legalists out or (2) separating oneself from them and finding a grace-oriented, classical dispensational fellowship of believers, going with the promise of Jesus in John 7:17: "Anyone is willing to do His will, he will know of the teaching, whether it is of God or *whether* I speak from Myself." God will lead you to such a fellowship or lead you to start one. Gather a few like-minded folks with you, meet in a home (remember you're not restricted to Sunday as the day), have one or two of the participants prepare a Bible study, sing a hymn or two, observe the Lord's Supper, discuss what you've heard, and enjoy each other.

This arrangement sounds odd to us, but it's what the early church did for 300 years before any buildings showed up. Besides the spiritual health and benefits, there are physical benefits, too: no salaries or bills to pay, no committees or constitutions to restrict who does what. For further insights into this in-a-home meeting read 1 Corinthians 14, remembering that the "prophets" are the teachers and remembering that the gift of tongues died out when the canon of Scripture was complete.

We've taken quite a journey since we began with the impact of the Mosaic Law. Now, lay down the law and "Grow in the grace and knowledge of our Lord and Savior Jesus Christ. To Him be the glory, both now and to the day of eternity. Amen" (2 Peter 3:18).

References

Adams, John. n.d. AZ Quotes. https://www.azquotes.com/quote/1325196

Adams, John. n.d. Goodreads. https://www.goodreads.com/quotes/1244732-remember-democracy-never-lasts-long-it-soon-wastes-exhausts-and

Adams, Samuel. n.d. Brainy Quote. https://www.brainyquote.com/quotes/samuel_adams_401817

Aldrich, Roy. 1959. "Causes for Confusion of Law and Grace." *Bibliotheca Sacra* 116, no. 463 (July). https://www.galaxie.com/article/bsac116-463-04

Aldrich, Roy. 1961. "The Mosaic Ten Commandments Compared to Their Restatements in the New Testament." Bibliotheca Sacra 118, no. 471 (July). https://www.galaxie.com/article/bsac118-471-06

Anderson, David R. 2010. *Free Grace Soteriology*. Maitland, FL: Xulon Press.

Armerding, Carl. 1961. "The Breastplate of Judgment." Bibliotheca Sacra 118, no. 469 (January). https://www.galaxie.com/article/bsac118-469-09

Armstrong, John H. 1998. "Editor's Introduction: Why Luther?" *Reformation and Revival* 7, no. 4 (Fall). https://www.galaxie.com/article/rar07-4-01

Arndt, William F., and F. Wilbur Gingrich. 1957. *A Greek-English Lexicon of the New Testament and Other Early Christian Literature* (3rd ed.). Chicago, IL: University of Chicago Press.

The Baptist Standard. 2013, January 10. Reprint of article from *The New York Times*, May 12, 1895.

Barna Group. 2015, February. "State of the Bible 2015." https://www.americanbible.org/uploads/content/State_of_the_Bible_2015_report.pdf

Bente, F., and Dau, W. H. T. 1921. "The Large Catechism by Martin Luther." In *Triglot Concordia: The Symbolical Books of the Evangelical Lutheran Church*, pp. 565 773. St. Louis, MO: Concordia Publishing House. Retrieved from Project Wittenberg, https://christian.net/pub/resources/text/wittenberg/luther/catechism/web/cat-09.html

Blackstone, William. *Commentaries on the Laws of England, vol. 1. 1765–1769* (1st ed.). Oxford: Clarendon Press.

Boetkke, Peter. 2018. "The Role of Private Property in a Free Society." In "Land Owner Rights and Environmental Law," February. https://travischarlessmith.com/the-role-of-private-property-in-a-free-society

Braman, Chuck. n.d. "The Political Philosophy of John Locke and Its Influence on the Founding Fathers and the Political Documents They Created." *Individualist Ideas*. https://individualistideas.com/political-philosophy-of-john-locke

Bunyan, John. 2003. *The Pilgrim's Progress*. New York: P. F. Collier & Son.

Busenitz, Irvin A. 2005. "The Reformers' Understanding of Paul and the Law." Masters Seminary Journal, 16, no. 2 (Fall). https://www.galaxie.com/article/tmsj16-2-03

Calvin, John. 1599. *Institutes of the Christian Religion.* London: Arnold Hatfield for Bonham Norton. https://ccel.org/ccel/calvin/institutes.toc.html

Carson, D. A. 2001. *From Sabbath to Lord's Day: A Biblical, Historical and Theological Investigation* (repr. ed.). Eugene, OR: Wipf and Stock.

CBS News. 2015, March 17. "Child Suicide Bombers." https://www.cbsnews.com/news/child-suicide-bombers-lara-logan-60-minutes

Chabad.org.

Clark, Micah. 2013, April 6. "Homosexual Activist Admits True Purpose of Battle Is to Destroy Marriage." Illinois Family Institute. https://illinoisfamily.org/homosexuality/homosexual-activist-admits-true-purpose-of-battle-is-to-destroy-marriage

Clement. n.d. *Ante-Nicene Fathers, Vol. IX: The Epistles of Clement Chapter XXXII.* https://st-takla.org/books/en/ecf/009/0090127.html

Cole, Stephen J. 2013, June. "Lesson 57: Why Jesus Hates Legalism." bible.org. https://bible.org/seriespage/lesson-57-why-jesus-hates-legalism-luke-1137-54

Constable, Thomas. n.d. "Expository Notes of Dr. Thomas Constable Malachi 3." *Bible Commentaries.* https://www.studylight.org/commentaries/dcc/malachi-3.html

Constitutional Rights Foundation. n.d. https://www.crf-usa.org

Crutchfield, Larry V. 1987a. "Rudiments of Dispensationalism in the Ante-Nicene Period: Part 1, Israel and the Church in the Ante-Nicene Fathers." *Bibliotheca Sacra* 144, no. 575: 254–277.

Crutchfield, Larry V. 1987b. "Rudiments of Dispensational-ism in the Ante-Nicene Period: Part 2: Ages and Dispensa-tions in the Ante-Nicene Fathers." *Bibliotheca Sacra* 144, no. 576: 377 402.

Dawkins, Richard. n.d. "Quotable Quotes." Goodreads. https://www.goodreads.com/quotes/23651-the-god-of-the-old-testa-ment-is-arguably-the-most

Deffinbaugh, Robert L. n.d. "Reasoning Through Romans: An Old Testament Illustration of Justification by Faith (Romans 4)." https://bible.org/seriespage/6-old-testament-illustration-justification-faith-romans-4

deMar, Gary. 2020. "Do Only Old Testament Laws Repeated in the New Testament Apply to Today?" *The American Vision*, February 18. https://americanvision.org/22266/do-only-old-testament-laws-repeated-in-the-new-testament-apply-today

Durant, Will. 1957. "The Reformation." In *The Story of Civili-zation*, vol. 6. New York: Simon and Schuster.

Encyclopedia Britannica. n.d. s.v. "Blue law." https://www.britannica.com/topic/blue-law

Erickson, Chris. 2010, March 16. "Salvation from the Perspec-tive of the Early Church Fathers." The Coming Home Network. https://chnetwork.org/2010/03/16/salvation-from-the-perspective-of-the-early-church-fathers

Family Foundation. n.d. https://www.familyfoundation.org/marriage

Federer, Bill. 2017, August 16. "Blackstone's *Commentaries* and the Revolution." Self Educated American. https://selfed-ucatedamerican.com/2017/08/16/blackstones-commentaries-revolution

Feinberg, Charles Lee. 1951. *Habakkuk, Zephaniah, Haggai, and Malachi: The Major Messages of the Minor Prophets*. "Thru the Bible." https://www.ttb.org/resources/study-guides/malachi-study-guide

Franklin, Benjamin. n.d. Goodreads. https://www.goodreads.com/quotes/9698261-democracy-is-two-wolves-and-a-lamb-voting-on-what

Friedenwald, Herbert. 1906. "Adams, John." http://www.jewishencyclopedia.com/articles/767-adams-john

Fruchtenbaum, Arnold. 2001. *Israelology: The Missing Link in Systematic Theology*. San Antonio, TX: Ariel Ministries.

Geisler, Norman. 1985. "A Premillennial View of Law and Government." *Bibliotheca Sacra* 142, no. 567. https://www.galaxie.com/article/bsac142-567-05

Gleason, Caroline. n.d. "The Chosen People of God: Mary Rowlandson's Captivity Narrative." Hanover College Department of History. https://history.hanover.edu/hhr/hhr4-2.html

Green, Joshua. 2005, October. "Roy and His Rock." *The Atlantic*. https://www.theatlantic.com/magazine/archive/2005/10/roy-and-his-rock/304264

Gundry, Stanley N. 1977. "Hermeneutics or Zeitgeist as the Determining Factor in Eschatologies?" *Journal of the Evangelical Theological Society* 20, no. 1 (Winter). https://www.galaxie.com/article/jets20-1-05

Hagerty, Barbara Bradley. 2009, September 26. "Swinging Chicken Ritual Divides Jews." NPR. https://www.npr.org/templates/story/story.php?storyId=113179433

Harless, Hal. 2003, July. "The Cessation of the Mosaic Covenant." *Bibliotheca Sacra* 160, no. 369. https://www.galaxie.com/article/bsac160-639-08

Hayek, F. A. n.d. Foundation for Economic Education. https://fee.org/articles/18-hayek-quotes-that-show-the-importance-of-liberty

Henry, Matthew. 2014. *Matthew Henry's Commentary on the Whole Bible* (6 vols.). Peabody, MA: Hendrickson Publishing Group.

Hillyer, Norman. 1970. "I Peter and the Feast of Tabernacles." *Tyndale Bulletin* 21, 39 70. https://legacy.tyndalehouse.com/tynbul/Library/TynBull_1970_21_02_Hillyer_1PeterFeastTabernacles.pdf

Holman Christian Standard Bible. 2009. Nashville, TN: Holman Bible Publishers.

Houdmann, S. Michael. n.d. "Who were Nadab and Abihu?" Got Questions? https://www.gotquestions.org/Nadab-and-Abihu.html

Irenaeus. (ca. 180 AD). *Against Heresies*.

Jefferson, Thomas. n.d. AZ Quotes. https://www.azquotes.com/quote/577414

Johnson, Eric L. 1998. "Who Are the Pharisees Today?" *Reformation and Revival* 7, no. 3 (Summer). https://www.galaxie.com/article/rar07-3-03

Johnson Jr., S. Lewis. 1963. "Studies in the Epistle to the Colossians Part VIII: The Paralysis of Legalism." *Bibliotheca Sacra* 120, no. 478 (April–June). https://www.galaxie.com/article/bsac120-478-02

Johnson Jr., S. Lewis. 2006. "Throw Out Those Legalists." *Emmaus Journal* vol. 15, no. 1 (Summer). https://www.galaxie.com/article/emj15-1-03

Josephus, Flavius. (Trans. William Whiston). 1841. *Antiquities of the Jews*. London: (private printing).

Kaiser, Jr., Walter. 1978. *The Promise-Plan of God: A Biblical Theology of the Old and New Testaments*. Grand Rapids, MI: Zondervan.

Lebovic, Matt. 2016, August 16. "Is the Hunt for Rembrandt's 'Galilee' Almost Over?" *The Times of Israel*. https://www.timesofisrael.com/is-the-hunt-for-rembrandts-stolen-galilee-almost-over

Lee, Arthur. 1782. "Quotes." Liberty Tree, September 23, 2013. http://libertytree.ca/quotes/Arthur.Lee.Quote.FEDD

Le Tourneau, R. G. 1968, February 23. "Foundations for Change" (speech at Founder's Banquet of Dallas Theological Seminary). *Bibliotheca Sacra* 125, no. 499 (July). https://www.galaxie.com/article/bsac125-499-04

Lewis, C. S. 1978. *The Lion, the Witch, and the Wardrobe*. New York: HarperCollins.

Liddell, Stephen. 2015, March 14. "A Brief History of Parliament." https://stephenliddell.co.uk/2015/03/14/a-brief-history-of-parliament

Lightfoot, J. B. (Translator). n.d. *The Didache*. https://christianhistoryinstitute.org/study/module/didache

Lightner, Robert P. 1985. "A Biblical Perspective on False Doctrine." *Bibliotheca Sacra*, 142, no. 565 (January). https://www.galaxie.com/article/bsac142-565-02

Long, Huey P. 1934. "Primary Source: Huey P. Long, 'Every Man a King' and 'Share Our Wealth." "Lumen," "The Great Depression Reader." https://courses.lumenlearning.com/ushistory2americanyawp/chapter/primary-source-huey-p-long-every-man-a-king-and-share-our-wealth-1934

Madison, James. 2018, February. In "Why Our Founders Feared Democracy." The Artful Dilettante. https://artfuldilettante.com/2018/02/04/why-our-founders-feared-democracy

Marcoe, Lauren. 2016, April 22. "Passover, most beloved Jewish holiday, explained." *USA Today*. https://www.usatoday.com/story/news/world/2016/04/22/passover-jewish-holiday-explained/83387514

Marx, Karl. n.d. Brainy Quote. https://www.brainyquote.com/quotes/karl_marx_157954

McBee, Richard. 2001. "Rembrandt in Berlin—Moses Breaking the Tablets of the Law." https://richardmcbee.com/writings/jewish-art-before-1800/item/rembrandt-in-berlin-moses-breaking-the-tablets-of-the-law

Merriam-Webster Collegiate Dictionary. 2003. 11th ed. s.v. "genocide."

Merriam-Webster.com. 2020. s.v. "anathema." https://www.merriam-webster.com/dictionary/anathema

Merrill, Eugene. 1991. "The Pentateuch." In A Biblical Theology of the Old Testament. Chicago: The Moody Bible Institute.

Moody, Dwight L. 1877. *New Sermons, Addresses, and Prayers*. New York: Henry S. Goodspeed.

My Jewish Learning. n.d. "Yom Kippur 101." https://www.myjewishlearning.com/article/yom-kippur-101

Otterman, Sharon. 2012. "Underwriting Abraham." *New York Times*, November 30. https://www.nytimes.com/2012/12/02/nyregion/underwriting-abraham-synagogues-offer-sponsorships-for-torah-texts.html

Pavao, Paul. n.d. "Clement of Rome." Christian History for Every Man. https://www.christian-history.org/clement-of-rome.html

Pentecost, J. Dwight. 1971. "The Purpose of the Law." *Bibliotheca Sacra* 128, no. 511 (July). https://www.galaxie.com/article/bsac128-511-04

Phillips, Casey. 2016, March 26. "Sixty Years Later, 'The Ten Commandments' Remains One of the Most Popular Biblical Films Ever Made." Chattanooga Free Press. https://www.timesfreepress.com/news/life/entertainment/story/2016/mar/26/sixty-years-later-ten-commandments-remains-on/356996

Plotz, H. 1996, June. "Man May Work From Sun to Sun but Woman's Work Is Never Done": A Short Note on Why the Issue of Household Work Is Important Socially, Economically, and Politically." *Family and Consumer Sciences*. https://onlinelibrary.wiley.com/doi/abs/10.1177/1077727X960244001

Pollard, Stephen. 2011, August 11. "The Breakdown of Family Life Has Led to Today's Anarchy." *Daily Express*. https://www.express.co.uk/comment/expresscomment/264228/The-breakdown-of-family-life-has-led-to-today-s-anarchy

Prager, Dennis. n.d. "The Ten Commandments: Introduction." assets.ctfassets.net/qnesrjodfi80/2Gmhiqz9kkM8iC62ay04yM/9ae1e6cf24d8297ba11c6dd668ea2feb/prager-ten_commandments_introduction-transcript.pdf

Preuschen, Erwin. 1900. In *The New Schaff-Herzog Encyclopedia of Religious Knowledge*. New York: Funk & Wagnalls.

Rand, Ayn. n.d. Brainy Quote. https://www.brainyquote.com/quotes/ayn_rand_125036

Random House Dictionary. 2017. s.v. "antinomian." https://www.dictionary.com/browse/antinomian?s=t

Rauser, Randal. 2014, January. "The Scandalous 'Sound of Music' and Other Favorite Examples of Christian Legalism." The Tentative Apologist. https://randalrauser.com/2014/01/the-scandalous-sound-of-music-and-other-favorite-examples-of-christian-legalism

Rich, Tracey R. 2011a. "Shabbat." *Judaism 101*. http://www.jewfaq.org/shabbat.htm

Rich, Tracey R. 2011b. "Yom Kippur." *Judaism 101*. http://www.jewfaq.org/holiday4.htm

Richard, Carl J. 2003. *Twelve Greeks and Romans Who Changed the World*. Lanham, MD: Rowman & Littlefield.

Richard, Carl J. 2016, August. Private correspondence with author.

Rome, Italy, Travel Guide, 2003 2016. "Michelangelo's Moses." https://www.rome.info/michelangelo/moses

Roosevelt, Theodore. 1910, August 31. "The New Nationalism." History for the Relaxed Historian. http://www.emersonkent.com/speeches/the_new_nationalism.htm

Rosengren, John. 2015, September 23. "Myth and Fact Part of Legacy from Sandy Koufax's Yom Kippur Choice." *Sports Illustrated*. https://www.si.com/mlb/2015/09/23/sandy-koufax-yom-kippur-1965-world-series

Ross, Allen. 2006, April 21. "The Religious World of Jesus: The Priests." bible.org. https://bible.org/seriespage/8-priests

Ruehring, Lauren Mitchell. n.d. "Michelangelo Sculptures." How Stuff Works. https://entertainment.howstuffworks.com/arts/artwork/michelangelo-sculptures10.htm

Ryrie, Charles. 1966. *Dispensationalism Today*. Chicago, IL: Moody Press.

Ryrie, Charles. 1986. *Basic Theology: A Popular Systematic Guide to Understanding Biblical Truth*. Wheaton, IL: SP Publications/Victor Books.

Ryrie, Charles. 1995. *Dispensationalism* (rev. ed.). Chicago, IL: Moody Press.

Schaff, Philip. n.d. "Calvin's Defence of the Death Penalty for Heretics." *History of the Christian Church*, 157. https://www.ccel.org/ccel/schaff/hcc8.iv.xvi.xxii.html

Schaff, Philip, ed. 1999. *St. Augustine: Confession, Life and Work*. Vol. 1: Early Church Fathers. [CD-ROM]. Dallas, TX: Galaxie Software/Prolegomena.

Scofield, C. I. 1909. *The Scofield Reference Bible*. New York: Oxford University Press.

Shahar, Yael. 2015, February 11. "The Ten Commandments." *Haaretz*. https://www.haaretz.com/jewish/the-ten-commandments-1.5416257

Shenoy, B. R. 1960, August 15. "East and West Berlin: A Study in Free vs Controlled Economy." https://www.libertarianism.org/publications/essays/east-west-berlin-study-free-vs-controlled-economy

Smith, Michael J. 2006. "The Role of the Pedagogue in Galatians." *Bibliotheca Sacra* 163, no. 650, 197 214. https://digitalcommons.liberty.edu/sor_fac_pubs/115

Sparknotes. n.d. "The Lion, the Witch, and the Wardrobe." https://www.sparknotes.com/lit/lion

Steinbeck, John. 2002. *The Grapes of Wrath*. New York: Penguin Putnam.

Stewart, James S. 1935. *A Man in Christ: The Vital Elements of St. Paul's Religion*. London: Hodder and Stoughton.

Taft, William Howard. n.d. AZ Quotes. https://www.azquotes.com/quote/675746

Tertullian. n.d. *Against Marcion*, book 5. New Advent. https://www.newadvent.org/fathers/03125.htm

Thayer, Joseph Henry. 1978. T*hayer's Greek-English Lexicon of the New Testament*. Grand Rapids, MI: Zondervan.

Thomas, W. H. Griffith. 1996. "A Voice from the Past: Priest or Prophet?" *Journal of the Grace Evangelical Society 9*, no. 1 (Spring). https://www.galaxie.com/article/jotges09-1-05?highlight=Priesthood

Torrence, Thomas. 1996. *The Doctrine of Grace in the Apostolic Fathers*. Eugene, OR: Wipf and Stock.

"The Truth About Palestinian Rock-Throwing." n.d. "Palestinian Child Indoctrination." https://thetruthaboutrockthrowing.wordpress.com/the-phenomenon/palestinian-child-indoctrination

Twain, Mark. 1904. *Notebook*. Directory of Mark Twain's Maxims, Quotations, and Various Opinions. http://www.twainquotes.com/God.html

Unger, Merrill F. 1950. "Archeology and the Religion of the Canaanites." *Bibliotheca Sacra* 107, no. 426 (April). https://www.galaxie.com/article/bsac107-426-04

Unger, Merrill F. 1964. *Unger's Bible Dictionary*. Chicago, IL: Moody Press.

Waltke, Bruce K. 2005. *The Book of Proverbs*. Grand Rapids, MI: William B. Eerdmans.

Waltke, Bruce K. 2011. "The Passover Ritual, Part 1: An Exposition of Exodus 12:1-14." *Emmaus Journal* 20, no. 1 (Summer). https://www.galaxie.com/article/emj20-1-04

Waltke, Bruce K. 2012a. "The Passover Ritual, Part 3: An Exposition of Exodus 12:1 14." *Emmaus Journal* 21, no. 2 (Winter). https://www.galaxie.com/article/emj21-2-03

Waltke, Bruce K. 2012b. "The Passover Ritual Parts 1 3." *Emmaus Journal*. https://www.galaxie.com/article/emj20-1-04

Watchtower. 1881. Nos. 10 & 11. *Reprints*, p. 301.

Wiersbe, Warren. 1981. *Be Complete*. Colorado Springs, CO: David C. Cook.

Winthrop, John. 1630. *A Modell of Christian Charity*. https://www.casa-arts.org/cms/lib/PA01925203/Centricity/Domain/50/A%20Model%20of%20Christian%20Charity.pdf

Yarbrough, Jean M. 2012, September. "Theodore Roosevelt: Progressive Crusader." The Heritage Foundation. https://www.heritage.org/political-process/report/theodore-roosevelt-progressive-crusader

Zacks, Richard. 2012, January 13. "How Dry We Aren't." *New York Times*. https://www.nytimes.com/2012/01/14/opinion/a-new-anti-alcohol-campaign-in-new-york.html

Zill, Nicholas, and W. Bradford Wilcox. 2016, September 12. "As the Family Goes, So Go the Public Schools." *National Review*. https://www.nationalreview.com/2016/09/public-school-performance-student-performance-married-parent-families-florida

About the Author

Dr. Michael D. Halsey is a co-founder of Grace Biblical Seminary and serves as its chancellor. He is a professor at both Grace Biblical Seminary and Cornerstone Bible Institute. He has taught on the graduate and undergraduate levels at Luther Rice College and in addition to teaching at Carver College. His Master of Theology degree as well as his Doctor of Ministry degree is from Dallas Theological Seminary. He is the author of *Truthspeak* and *The Gospel of Grace and Truth: A Theology of Grace from the Gospel of John*. His radio program, "The Rest of the Story," can be heard on graceglobalradio.org. Dr. Halsey enjoys reading ancient history and correlating the events and culture of the 1st century AD with the New Testament. He and his wife, Mary, live in a suburb 25 miles south of Atlanta.

Other Titles from Grace Acres Press

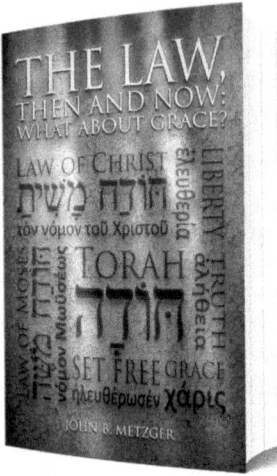

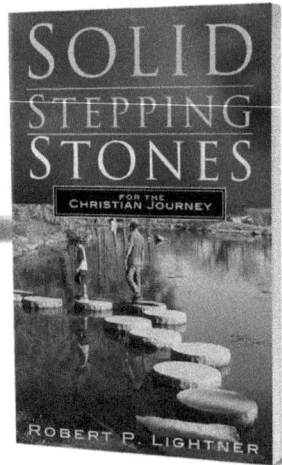

THE LAW,
THEN AND NOW:
WHAT ABOUT GRACE?

LAW OF CHRIST
LIBERTY
TORAH
SET FREE GRACE

JOHN B. METZGER

LIFE
BEFORE
DEATH

A Restored, Regenerated,
and Renewed Life

IAN LEITCH

Foreword by Joseph M. Stowell

SOLID
STEPPING
STONES
FOR THE
CHRISTIAN JOURNEY

ROBERT P. LIGHTNER

Other Titles from Grace Acres Press

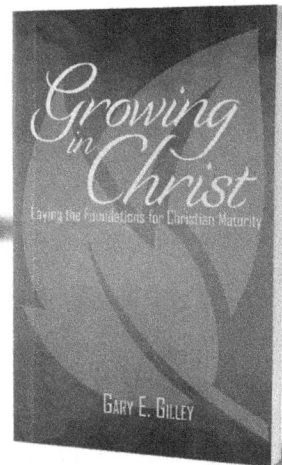

LIVING
THROUGH THE
STRUGGLE
1 Peter's Lessons for Today

CHAD NIGHTINGALE

For
THOU
Art With Me

*Biblical Help for the Terminally
Ill and Those Who Love Them*

Bruce A. Baker, PhD

Growing
in
Christ
Laying the Foundations for Christian Maturity

GARY E. GILLEY

Available at GraceAcresPress.com
or wherever books are sold.

217

Growing Your Faith One Page at a Time

Resources for Cultivating Joy

Small Group—Sunday School—Personal Study

GRACE ACRES PRESS

CULTIVATING JOY

Grace Acres Press

GraceAcresPress.com

www.ingramcontent.com/pod-product-compliance
Lightning Source LLC
Chambersburg PA
CBHW060046100426
42742CB00014B/2720